Music For Middlebrows

About the Author

Des Keogh was born in Birr, County Offaly. He was at Glenstal Priory (now Abbey) School, UCD (BA in French and German), King's Inns (BL) and the University of Munich. For two and a half years he worked for Arthur Guinness in Dublin and Belfast. Since 1963 he has been a professional actor, entertainer and broadcaster.

His work on stage, television and film has brought him to many parts of the world including Great Britain, the USA, Canada, Australia and the West Indies.

His home is in Dublin where he enjoys the company of his wife Geraldine and his daughter Oonagh (both violinists), his dog Presto and his cat Pamina (sometimes referred to as Offenbach and Debussy). He himself still has ambitions to be a musician like the others.

Music for

Middlebrows

Des Keogh

Foreword by Maureen Potter
Illustrations by Alan Cotsini

ASHFIELD
Press

Published by Ashfield Press
an imprint of *Blackhall Publishing*,
26 Eustace Street
Dublin 2

e-mail: blackhall@tinet.ie

ISBN: 1 901658 17 1   pbk
            1 901658 18 X   hbk

A catalogue record for this book is available from the British Library.

Printed in Ireland by
Betaprint Ltd

Contents

The Mid-Romantics (1850-1880)

Acknowledgements

Some books have pages and pages of acknowledge-ments and this one might too, if only I knew the names of all the people listening to *Music for Middlebrows*. There must be a large number – otherwise I wouldn't be still on the air. RTÉ does not encourage people to sit in studios talking to themselves. So, thank you all for listening.

I have mentioned elsewhere my two main RTÉ producers but there were occasional others and there were disc-jockeys, sound-operators, the ever-obliging staff in the record library and various "heads" who were helpful. My thanks to you all.

A couple of people must be mentioned by name. My publisher, Gerard O'Connor, took this on faith when it was just a heap of hand-written, illegible sheets of paper. Thank you, Gerry, for taking such a leap in the dark. I hope your reward will not only be in Heaven!

I have no words to express the admiration I have for Maureen Potter who has been characteristically warm and generous in her foreword. Thank you, Mo, for doing me such an honour.

My thanks to Alan Corsini for his delightful illus-trations, both on the cover and throughout the book. I hope you enjoy these as much as I do.

Finally, this would not have happened at all with-out Ríona MacNamara. The book was her brain-child a few years ago and when the going got tough early this summer she encouraged, counselled and cajoled me to bring it to completion. Ríona, you're the tops!

To Geraldine and Oonagh
(the "Dynamic Duo")
with all my love

Foreword

This book deserves an overture not a foreword. However, my talent for composition consisted of thinking up excuses to get out of school in time for matinée performances at the Theatre Royal or the Queen's. So if not an overture why not a fanfare? I have been a Des Keogh fan for many years so it is an honour to provide the foreword for this fascinating book.

Despite his youthful appearance and attitude Des is a man of considerable theatrical experience. It stretches back to the days of Hilton Edwards and Micheál Mac Líammóir at The Gate and onward to many successes in America. The revues starring Rosaleen Linehan and Des were treasures to be cherished and are sadly missed. As a result, today's politicians sleep more peacefully in their beds, or in somebody's bed. The Celtic Tiger too enjoys the forest of the night. Sic transit gloria swansong!

I worked with Des in pantomime, summer revue and O'Casey. He is the consummate professional, most supportive and giving, and very good company on and off the stage. A great comfort to me too was that he gets even more nervous than me before every performance. He has no need to be nervous about this book. I feel sure it will be as successful as *Music for Middlebrows* has been for 30 years.

The book has delightful tit bits and anecdotes about so many composers and their music. It makes them less formidable, more human, more accessible. Next time Leontyne Price completes my happy Christmas by singing 'O Holy Night' I will impress my guests by saying "that dates back to Adam, of course". (See page 88.)

I was delighted to see George Gershwin rightly included among the greats. There was much written about him on the centenary of his birth and one story struck me as being both funny and very brave. During the last war when the Germans were making propaganda broadcasts directed at little Denmark the Danish underground interrupted them by playing 'It Ain't Necessarily So'. George Gershovitz would have appreciated that.

I must take issue with one sentence in the introduction. Des writes "this is a book for people who, like myself, love music but don't know a great deal about it". WRONG!! He knows a great deal about music, he has proved it in 30 years of *Music for Middlebrows* and once again in this enthralling book. I loved it.

Maureen Potter
October 1998

*I*ntroduction

This is a book for people like myself, who love music but don't know a great deal about it. I was hooked on music from the moment I first heard a symphony orchestra. I was about twelve when a musical aunt brought me to the Theatre Royal to hear the Hallé Orchestra, conducted by Sir John Barbirolli. That was not the occasion when those eminent musicians were introduced by Dublin's Lord Mayor as 'Sir John Barbolly and his band.' My aunt's name was Mary Keogh ('Chummie' to family and close friends). She was organist at Haddington Road church, where I later deputised for her on occasions, earning the princely sum of four shillings. That was not to be sneezed at in those student days – it was enough to get me three pints of Guinness. Chummie was also a renowned trainer of school choirs, and was so successful for years at the Feis Ceol that it was known to some as the Feis Keogh.

I took piano lessons right through my school days and also when I was a student at UCD. I was lucky to have the legendary Lily Huban as my teacher in Dublin. I'm sure she tolerated me as a favour to my aunt, because I always arrived with profuse apologies for not having practised. I still play the piano a bit, but my greatest performances are given when I am asleep or daydreaming. My favourite fantasy is striding out onto the stage of a great concert hall, where the most distinguished conductor and magnificent orchestra in the world are waiting for me. I acknowledge the rapturous applause of the capacity audience while peeling off the white gloves. Then I seat myself at the Steinway and launch myself into the Tchaikovsky or Rachmaninov with accustomed panache. (I once dreamt that I was onstage in Carnegie Hall, and when I woke up I was – though only telling jokes!)

I was very fortunate as a student to spend a year

at the University of Munich. I was supposed to be studying German literature, but spent more time in concert and beer halls than in the academic variety. I heard wonderful music in Munich – there was such a range that I was spoiled for choice. Back in Dublin I went to hear the Radio Éireann Symphony Orchestra at every opportunity. There were free concerts in those days (them was days, Joxer!). For some time I admired from a distance the lovely young leader of the orchestra, Geraldine O'Grady. I met her in 1965, when I was introducing a television programme called *Melody Fair*. It was love at first meeting and we were married a few months later. There was a rumour going around for a while that I was married to Rosaleen Linehan – we did have a close working relationship, but it was a case of "just good friends". I once introduced Geraldine from the stage of the National Concert Hall as "the loveliest violinist I have ever lived with", and was attacked on the way out by a lady who said that Rosaleen should never have married me!

But on to *Music for Middlebrows*. In 1968 I went to Kevin Roche, then Head of Light Music at RTÉ with a programme idea and a title. Kevin liked both and scheduled an initial series of thirteen weeks, which has turned into 30 years. My idea was to present all the great melodies from classical music in an informal, layman's way. I wanted to communicate as best I could to the listeners my own great joy in listening to the classics. I found as I went along that people liked to hear little tit-bits and anecdotes about the composers and the music. Over the years I have received hundreds of letters from people all over Ireland, telling me how much they have enjoyed listening to my programmes. I may not have been able to answer all the letters, but I have certainly appreciated them, and have always taken listeners' requests into account when compiling the programmes.

I have been extraordinarily fortunate in having had only two main producers of *Music for Middlebrows*. The first was John Carolan, a dear man who sadly died recently. Fiach was succeeded in 1985 by Fiach Ó Broin, who is still with me. He tries me sorely with his jokes which run the gamut from A to B (abysmal to brilliant) but he is a great friend. I love him and would not have survived without him.

One of the great pleasures of *Music for Middlebrows* has been my association with the RTÉ Concert Orchestra and its principal conductor Proinnsias O'Duinn. Proinnsias has always been most co-operative and the concerts in Dublin and elsewhere with these marvellous musicians have always been very popular. I enjoy the opportunity of presenting classical music to a live audience in the same non-academic way as I do on radio, and it's a thrill to get the enthusiastic feedback. I really hope that these concerts will continue for many years.

For the purposes of this book, I have chosen 40 top middlebrow composers – by which I mean those composers who have written the most melodious and accessible music – and looked at their personalities and music in more detail than the other 50 or so. You may well question my choice – no two people could agree on something like this – but they are, in my opinion, the most popular if not necessarily the greatest. I have also divided them up into periods and looked at them chronologically as far as possible. It is my sincere hope that you will enjoy reading this volume, and that it will add to your pleasure in listening not only to my programme, but to all the other music programmes on radio. Above all, I hope you will be encouraged to sample the delights of live concerts, and with the great work being done by RTÉ and by the Arts Council, Music Network and the Music Association of Ireland, there is more music available throughout the country than there ever was. Long may it continue, and if music be the food of love, read on!

The Baroque Period (1600-1750)

The beginning is supposed to be a very good place to start, but I'm not going to start at the very beginning, because middle-brow music doesn't go back quite that far. We start in the 17th century, the earliest member of our Top 40 being Vivaldi, born in 1678, with Bach and Handel, both born in 1685, hard on his heels. This is the period which has been called 'baroque' and covers about 150 years, from 1600 to 1750. The term 'baroque' was not invented for music, but for painting and architecture. It actually means, in French, 'bizarre' or 'grotesque' but was applied to the highly decorated style (full of curves) of the German and Austrian buildings of the period. By association it has come to be applied to the music of the same period.

How does this music differ from that of other eras? Well, one big difference was in the rhythm, which was given much more emphasis than in later times. The music of Vivaldi, Bach and Handel always had a strong, steady rhythm. There was melody in abundance, but it was embellished with trills and ornaments. It was often accompanied by a bass line (known as continuo), which was not written out note for note but which could be improvised by the musicians involved, who played organ or harpsichord, with cello, double-bass or even bassoon. Baroque music had other characteristics as well, but I don't want to give you the wrong idea by becoming academic at this early stage (or at any stage!). Generally, the music of this period was clean-lined, extravagantly decorated and rhythmically strict. In fact, it was much influenced by dances popular at the time – minuet, gavotte, bourrée, rigaudon, sarabande, gigue – but there was always an air as well, to give the feet a break. These dances all put together made up the orchestral suite, which was very popular in this pre-symphony period.

Also very popular at this time was the concerto. There were two kinds: the solo concerto, featuring a single soloist accompanied by a group of musicians and the concerto grosso ('big concerto'), which featured a small group of soloists with a larger orchestral group. The basic idea was a musical dialogue between soloists and orchestra, with the solo parts being usually more florid and assertive. Early purveyors of the concerto were the Venetian Albinoni (1671-1751), the German Telemann (1681-1767) and, of course, our Big Three.

Opera was also developing at this time. The earliest operatic composer of note was Monteverdi (1567-1643) and in the Baroque Period there were Lully and Rameau in France, Purcell and, above all, Handel in England.

If you want to sample the delights of the Baroque period Deutsche Gramophon have a wonderful 'Mad About...' series of compilation CDs, one of which is *Mad About Baroque*. Baroque music has become very popular in recent times and there's a vast number of CD compilations to choose from.

ANTONIO VIVALDI
(1675-1741)

Antonio Vivaldi was known as the "red priest" because of his enormous red beard. He suffered from asthma and soon after his ordination had to give up saying mass. There was also the problem that he seemed unable to resist the attractions of the opposite sex.

Vivaldi was born in Venice and was first taught music by his father, a violinist of St Mark's Chapel. For 36 years he was musical major-domo of one of the big girls' schools, originally known in Venice as 'hospitals', that had been established by religious organisations for the education – especially in music – of orphans and the children of poverty-stricken or unmarried parents. A contemporary description exists of these pupils:

> *They are reared at public expense and trained solely to excel in music. And they do sing like angels and play the violin, flute, organ, oboe, violincello, bassoon...each concert is given by about 40 girls. I assure you that there is nothing so charming as to see a young and pretty nun in her white robe with a spray of pomegranate flowers in her hair, conducting the orchestra and beating time with all the precision imaginable.*

Such was Vivaldi's domain. One of his responsibilities was to compose concertos for the girls – often as many as two a month. He is credited with about 450 concertos for every conceivable instrument and combination of instruments, though the majority are for one or more violins. He also wrote an enormous amount of vocal music at the Pietà Conservatory – motets, masses, vespers, all sorts of choral works. Vivaldi was bound by contract to fulfil his obligations even when he was not in residence and he did travel a lot and indulge in various extra-mural activities.

Vivaldi was also active in the operatic field. He had about 40 operas produced, not only in Venice but also in Rome, Florence, Verona and other places. He acted as his own impresario, engaging the singers and dancers, paying the bills and keeping a calculating eye on the box office.

One story about Vivaldi tells how he was suspended from his priestly functions by the Inquisition because, while celebrating mass, he had rushed off the altar to write down a musical idea before it escaped him. He himself, however, claimed that the choice to leave the priesthood was his own, prompted by illness. He also claimed that he was very well behaved at the Conservatory:

> *I have been Maestro della Pietà for over 30 years with never a scandal.*

Hmmm! He travelled very little during the last six years of his life but died in Vienna in poor circumstances.

Vivaldi holds a place in musical history as a master of the concerto and Stravinksy was being really snide to say that he wrote the same concerto a hundred times. Bach, however, was definitely an admirer and arranged a number of Vivaldi's concertos for keyboard. Vivaldi was a fantastically fluent composer and wrote music of irrepressible charm. His most famous piece, of course, is *The Four Seasons*, which must be one of the most frequently played classical compositions in the world.

Vivaldi – A Middlebrow Mix

The Four Seasons and Other Concertos

If Vivaldi did write the same concerto a hundred times, there are still 350 that are original and that ought to be enough for anybody.

The Four Seasons

Vivaldi is primarily known as a composer of concertos, though he wrote in virtually every musical form, from sonata to opera. He was a violinist himself and most of his concertos are for strings but there are also some for oboe, bassoon, flute and practically every other instrument. *The Four Seasons* is a set of four miniature concertos for violin, strings and continuo. Each concerto follows quite closely the lines of an 'illustrative sonnet' written by Vivaldi himself.

In the opening concerto, joyful birdsong heralds the arrival of spring – 'Spring has returned again and festively the birds salute him with their joyous song.' In the second movement, shepherds sleep peacefully in a meadow while the viola gives an impression of a barking dog until finally the shepherds indulge in a graceful dance. Vivaldi's idea of summer is one of torrid heat. The turtledove and goldfinch answer the cuckoo's call, but suddenly the wind changes and we have swarms of flies and insects, followed by a fierce storm with hailstones battering the crops. Happily, when it comes to autumn, the crops seem to have survived – 'With songs and dances, country folk cheer, the satisfaction of a fruitful harvest'. Then everyone falls into a drink-befuddled sleep but they are aroused at dawn by hunting horns and the cry of tally-ho – the chase is on. Finally we have the icy winds of winter, but in the exquisite largo we have the reassurance that we can keep warm by the blazing hearth while raindrops fall harmlessly on the window ledge outside. The recording by the English hotshot Nigel Kennedy (now simply Kennedy) a few years ago was very popular, but there are umpteen to choose from.

In addition to *The Four Seasons*, the twelve main concertos of Opus 3 are recommended. These are known as 'L'Estro Armonico' ('Harmonious Inspiration') and are for one, two, three and four violins, sometimes with cello and orchestra. The best thing to do with Vivaldi, I think, is to go for a 'Best of' CD which will give you a selection of concertos. They're all quite short with two lively outer movements and usually a serene, soothing melody between them. The wind players are well catered for, with concertos for flute, oboe, trumpet and bassoon. One beauty that we've had a few times on *Music for Middlebrows* is 'Concerto in C for Mandolin' (R425).

Gloria in D

There are many famous Glorias from masses by famous composers, but this independent one by Vivaldi is very popular and is a must if you are into that sort of liturgical music. There are many recordings to choose from. If you enjoy this you could also look up a 'Kyrie' (R587) and a 'Credo' (R591) – R numbers for Vivaldi are cataloguing numbers, just as K is for Mozart.

JOHANN SEBASTIAN BACH
(1685-1750)

A child wrote in an essay: "Bach was a master of the Passion and had twenty children." Robert Schumann said of him, "Music owes as much to Bach as Christianity to Christ." This is typical of the superlatives used by writers, critics and fellow composers in their assessments of Johann Sebastian. What do middlebrows think of him? Well! There are a number of pieces that fall into the middlebrow category but overall the majority would think of Bach as a bit on the highbrow side. Still, no book on music could be written without acknowledging the enormous contribution made by this genius, "the most stupendous miracle in all music", to quote Wagner. If you don't feel like sitting through the great choral works, one way to enjoy the wondrous melodies of Bach is to listen to orchestral transcriptions of his works. The great conductor Leopold Stokowski specialised in this and with the mighty Philadelphia Orchestra brought Bach to a much wider audience. Ideally, though, you must experience the 'Mass in B Minor', the *St Matthew Passion* and those other incredible compositions *in toto* and preferably in a great church or concert hall.

Bach was prolific in more senses than one. His first wife Maria Barbara bore him seven children but she died tragically in 1720 at a very early age. Bach was not even at home when she died, and was devastated when he returned to Cöthen to find that she had died and been buried during his absence. Nevertheless it was little over a year later when he married the 20-year-old Anna Magdalena Wilcken. His second marriage was as happy as his first and the union produced 13 more children, not all of whom survived infancy. Of all his children four followed him into the music business.

Music was a tradition in the Bach family. For four generations before Johann Sebastian, the Bach men had been musical craftsmen as others had been stonemasons or builders. In the 17th and 18th centuries, over 50 Bachs held positions of musical responsibility in the courts and towns of German-speaking Europe.

The compositions of Bach can be divided roughly into their chronological periods: the Weimar organ period, the Cöthen chamber music and orchestral period and the Leipzig oratorio period.

The organ was Bach's first great love and his first professional jobs were as an organist. He spent time at Armstadt and Mülhausen and then, in 1708, he went to Weimar as court organist and chamber musician to the reigning Duke Wilhelm Ernst. He won a reputation as the finest organist in Europe and composed here the majority of his organ masterpieces. On one occasion an organ-playing contest was arranged between Bach and the highly regarded Marchand, organist to Louis XV, but the Frenchman got cold feet and left town before the time appointed for the head-to-head. After nine years Bach moved to Cöthen but only after a big row with the Duke, who refused to release him from his engagements and actually locked him up for a while. However, in 1717 Bach settled in Cöthen and the period here is distinguished by a steady stream of wonderful chamber music, orchestral suites, sonatas and concertos of all sorts, including the famous Brandenburg concertos dedicated to Christian Ludwig, Margrave of Brandenburg. His main responsibility here was to conduct the court orchestra in which his employer Prince Leopold himself played.

In 1723 Bach was appointed Director of Music at the St Thomas Church and School at Leipzig and he remained there for almost the last 30 years of his life. His duties were to supervise the choirboys' musical activities and to compose, rehearse and conduct music for the city's churches. His output of cantatas was prodigious as he composed one for each Sunday and holy day throughout the year. Towering above these were the 'Mass in B Minor' and the *St Matthew Passion* – regarded by many as the two greatest religious works of all time.

Bach was not as celebrated during his lifetime as other composers like Handel. He did not travel much but kept his musical nose to the grindstone, turning out the wondrous works which were expected of him. Most of his works were not published until after his death, so were only heard locally. For 80 or so years after his death the musical public heard very little of his work either. It was Mendelssohn who changed all that. He dusted off the *St Matthew Passion* and in 1829 conducted its first public performance since Bach's day. Other revivals followed, plus performances of previously unpublished works and by the middle of the century Bach was hailed worldwide as a giant.

He was stricken with blindness toward the end of his life. An operation aggravated the condition and he suffered a paralytic stroke. His death and burial in Leipzig in 1750 went largely unnoticed by the public.

Bach – A Middlebrow Mix

Concerto for Two Violins in D Minor

Bach was not only the greatest keyboard musician of his day, he was also an accomplished violinist and violist, having learned from his father. He was among the admirers of the Venetian master Vivaldi and, during his period of employment at Weimar, Bach transcribed ten of Vivaldi's concertos for keyboard instruments. In his own string concertos, while following the basic form set by Vivaldi, Bach varied and developed it a great deal. Unique among his works is the concerto for two violins and string orchestra. Here the two soloists do not compete in any way, they are in complete accord with each other and with the other strings. The form is that of the Italian concerto. a lively first movement and a brisk rondo to close with, in between, one of Bach's most remarkable creations, a profound largo in which the two solo violins intertwine magically.

That this is one of my favourite works by Bach has of course nothing to do with the fact that I have enjoyed hearing it performed by the two violinists to whom this book is dedicated – my wife and daughter.

Toccata and Fugue in D Minor for Organ

This is perhaps the best known of all organ works – a thrilling piece which I had the temerity to attempt at school. James Mason as Captain Nemo made a better job of it in the film *20,000 Leagues Under The Sea*. The Stokowski orchestral version was featured in the Disney masterpiece *Fantasia*.

The word toccata comes from the Latin toccare, 'to touch'. It originated in the 16th century and was applied principally to show-off pieces for keyboard players. In this great organ composition, Bach's toccata is like a great prelude with all the stops out and it is followed by a fugue, a term derived from the Latin word fuga, meaning 'flight'. A fugue is a bit like a canon, with the same tune chasing itself, but fugues are far more complex and can take diversions and investigate all sorts of lanes and byways. Come to think of it, I could never really play a fugue – I haven't enough fingers!

Brandenburg Concerto No. 2

This is the most popular of the six concertos written for and named after the Margrave of Brandenburg. The concertos are for different solo groups and strings and this one features trumpet, flute, oboe and violin. The outer movements are bright and breezy with dangerously high trumpet parts and the middle movement is a heartfelt song highlighting violin and oboe.

Suite No. 3 in D for Orchestra

This work was composed for a large ensemble of strings, oboes, trumpets and timpani. Where there are trumpets and drums in Bach's work, it usually means that the piece was written for a festive occasion and often intended to be heard out of doors. The suite opens with an impressive overture, followed by the celebrated air which was arranged by violinist August Wilhelmj and is known separately as 'Air on the G-String'. Then there are three lively dances so typical of the Baroque orchestral suite.

Cantatas

A cantata is a poem or text set to music, consisting of airs and choruses with orchestral accompaniment. The text can be either religious or secular but the church cantata is particularly well known, mainly due to Bach, who wrote cantatas for all sorts of church occasions and religious feasts. During his years in Leipzig, he was expected to compose a 30-minute cantata every week. There are three that particularly stand out.

Jesu, Joy of Man's Desiring

This is the last movement of Cantata No. 147 ('Heart and Mouth and Deed and Life') and was composed for the Feast of the Visitation. Around the main tune Bach entwines a faster accompanying melody which has become very well known. Originally for choir and small orchestra, it has been arranged for all sorts of instruments – possibly the best loved version is the arrangement for piano solo popularised by Dame Myra Hess during World War II.

Wachet Auf ('Sleepers Awake')

This comes from Cantata No. 140, which was written for the 27th Sunday after Trinity. The Gospel reading for the day is the parable of the wise and foolish virgins and essentially this is a wedding cantata representing the union of Christ and the human soul. The chorale is a joyous work with a flowing melody which sums up the devotional theme of the whole cantata.

Sheep May Safely Graze

This glorious melody comes from Secular Cantata No. 208 and was written for the birthday of Bach's employer at Weimar in 1716. As the name implies it is a pastoral scene-painting and is heard in various arrangements, one being for a ballet by Sir William Walton.

GEORGE FRIDERIC HANDEL
(1685-1789)

Handel was baptised Georg Friedrich Händel in Saxony, Germany but he later decided to become an Englishman and anglicised his name, though he never lost his German accent. He was born in the same year as Bach and was similarly gifted as a keyboard player, becoming a renowned virtuoso on both organ and harpsichord.

When he was twenty, Handel had great success with an Italian opera and decided to turn his talents to composing for the stage. He worked in Italy for four years, absorbing the Italian operatic style, which was all the rage at the time. He then went to London where he lived for the rest of his life. Between 1710 and 1740 he composed operas at a rate averaging more than one major work per year. These were staged at the Queen's Theatre in the Haymarket, which he also managed, and they were the talk of the town.

Handel was an important personage in London, worshipped by many but, not surprisingly, disliked by some. He was proud (arrogant, perhaps), straightforward (or rude), and subservient to no man (not even the monarch). He became a kind of unofficial Master of the Royal Music and composed special works for state occasions, the two most famous being *Water Music* and *Music for the Royal Fireworks*.

During the 1730s, the fashion for Italian opera waned. John Gay's *The Beggar's Opera* set a new fashion for English theatre entertainment – a fashion less showy and artificial. Handel even found himself and his florid Italian-style operas being lampooned. He saw the writing on the wall and, being a resourceful man, turned to a new musical form: the oratorio.

The English passion for oratorio is largely due to Handel. Every year between 1738 and 1751 he produced at least one. He had Bible stories dramatised (in English), then set them to music, incorporating virtuoso solo arias and, of course, the majestic choruses which became their trademark. The orchestral accompaniments, too, are thrilling and Handel often included as interludes organ solos or concertos recalling the virtuosity of his youth. The new recipe brought him another twenty years of public acclaim. The most celebrated oratorio of all is *Messiah*, first performed in Dublin in 1741.

Apart from the oratorios, Handel's most respected works are the orchestral concerti grossi. The concerto grosso was a popular form for about a hundred years between 1650 and 1750, often featuring several solo instruments and an orchestra of strings and harpsichord.

Handel never married and had no public love life. He made up for it by indulging himself with good food and drink. He had a violent temper, but also a sense of humour and was able to laugh at himself. When a friend remarked on the poor music being played at the Vauxhall Gardens, he replied, "You are right, sir, it is very poor stuff. I thought so myself when I wrote it."

One person who certainly didn't think Handel's music was poor was Beethoven who said, among other things, that:

Handel is the unattained master of all masters...he is the greatest, the most solid of composers...in the future I shall write after the manner of my grand master Handel.

An English critic wrote: "He did bestride our musical world like a Colossus." When he died, after seven years of blindness, Handel was buried with appropriate pomp in Westminster Abbey.

Handel – A Middlebrow Mix

Messiah

Handel's *Messiah* is probably the most popular of all oratorios. We, in Ireland, have a special affection for it, of course, because the first performance was given in Dublin on 13 April 1742. An advertisement in the *Dublin News-Letter* broke the news:

On Monday the 12th April will be performed at the Musick Hall in Fishamble Street Mr Handel's New Grand Oratorio called 'Messiah'.

There was such a crush at the rehearsal that the papers had to print a special plea in advance of the première. It was urgently hoped, the notices said, that ladies would be pleased to come without hoops and that gentlemen would similarly leave their swords at home, thereby increasing the space available in the hall. *Messiah* continues to draw crowds in the city of its birth – particularly the annual performances by Our Lady's Choral Society.

Handel composed *Messiah* in 25 days and it is said that when he had completed the 'Hallelujah Chorus' his servant found him at his writing table staring into space as he whispered:

> *I did think I did see all Heaven before me and the great God Himself.*

The text, compiled by Charles Jenners, draws on both the Old and the New Testaments to tell, in extremely compressed form, the story of the life of Christ. There are four soloists – soprano, alto, tenor and bass, each being given a chance to shine. Part I presents God's plan to redeem the world through a Saviour, and tells the story of the Nativity. The alto has two of the most popular arias in the first part – 'O thou that tellest good tidings to Zion' and 'He shall feed His flock like a shepherd'. Also noteworthy is the chorus 'For unto us a child is born'.

The theme of Part II is the victory of Christ over sin and the perpetuation of His kingdom on earth. Highlights are the alto aria 'He was despised' and the chorus 'All we like sheep'. At the end of this part comes the most famous of all oratorio pieces – the 'Hallelujah Chorus'. It is the custom that the audience stands for this chorus. We are told that the practice was started by King George II, who was so impressed when he first heard it that he spontaneously rose to his feet.

The concluding part concerns the promise of redemption, resurrection and eternal life. The soprano has the wonderful aria 'I know that my redeemer liveth', the bass gets to sing 'The trumpet shall sound' and all ends with the great 'Amen' chorus.

Water Music

Handel's *Water Music* was written for a royal party on the Thames in the summer of 1717. It was commissioned by King George I or on his behalf, as the King was in need of some good PR at the time. His advisers thought that a display of magnificence might improve his image. He had come direct from Germany to be King of England but his one little handicap was that he spoke no English. He wasn't too pleased with Handel, who had left his court in Hanover to come to England, but composer and King soon made up – who wouldn't forgive a man who could write that sort of music for your picnic? The King and his co-horts listened from the royal barge on the way up to Chelsea for supper while an ensemble of 50 musicians played Mr Handel's wonderful music on another. His Majesty was delighted and the non-unionised musicians had to repeat the whole thing on the way back.

There were 21 pieces in the original *Water Music* and they are now usually divided into three separate suites depending on the instrumentation. The 'Suite in F' has the most instruments and features French horns as well as oboes, bassoon and strings. The 'Suite in D' is the original one with trumpets and contains the celebrated hornpipe. The 'Suite in G' is the lightweight, with flute and other woodwind, but no brass. The first two suites are clearly open-air music and were probably played on the barge, but the third sounds as if it may have been designed to accompany the King's indoor meal at Chelsea.

It would be remiss not to mention also the *Music for the Royal Fireworks*. This was commissioned by a King George but this time by George II. He ordered a great deal of public entertainment to celebrate the end of the war of the Austrian succession and the signing of the Treaty of Aix-la-Chapelle. There was to be a huge fireworks display, accompanied by Handel's music, scored for as many martial instruments as possible. Handel complied with the King's wishes and composed a huge instrumental showpiece for brass and woodwind. Strings were added later and, as in the case of the *Water Music*, there is a very popular suite arranged by Sir Hamilton Harty for full symphony orchestra.

The actual fireworks display in 1749 was a fiasco. A gunner was killed priming the guns for the royal salute and, when the fireworks finally condescended to go off, they set fire to the specially constructed victory pavilion. The music, at least, was magnificent.

Other Handel Must-Hears

There is so much wonderful music by Handel that it's difficult to pull out the very best. However, there are some middlebrow musts. The piece known to all and sundry as Handel's *Largo* started life as a song ('Ombra mai fu') in the opera *Xerxes*. It is a hymn extolling the virtues of a plane tree. 'Where'er you walk' is a very popular tenor aria from the opera *Semele*. 'The Arrival of the Queen of Sheba' is a wonderful orchestral interlude in the oratorio *Solomon* – deliciously scored for oboe and strings. 'See the conquering hero comes' is a splendid chorus from the oratorio *Judas Maccabaeus*; 'Let the bright seraphim' is an inspiring piece for soprano with trumpet obbligato from the oratorio *Samson* and the minuet from the opera *Berenice* is a delight.

OTHER BAROQUE NOTEWORTHIES

Johann Pachelbel
(1653-1706)

This German composer held various important positions as organist in Vienna and in his native Germany. His keyboard compositions were an important influence on his younger contemporary Johann Sebastian Bach. However, his name is perpetuated by one piece known as 'Canon '. A canon is a piece of music where the same notes are repeated, started at different times. (It's not difficult: think of 'Three blind mice'. One person starts and when they get to the line 'See how they run', the next person starts off with 'Three blind mice' and so on, everything fitting in perfectly.) As with many popular classical pieces, it became well known through television: it was used to great effect in Carl Sagan's ground-breaking series *Cosmos*, which introduced many types of music to a whole new audience.

Tomaso Albinoni
(1671-1751)

Albinoni was one of the Venetian composers who contributed to making the Venice of that period one of the artistic centres of Europe. He wrote over 50 operas and about 100 concertos of all sorts, but he is best known to middlebrows for one piece of which he probably composed only the bare melody. This was discovered early in this century by an Italian musicologist called Giazotto, who expanded and developed it into the piece we know and love today as the 'Adagio for Organ and Strings', an exquisite piece of sustained melody. Film buffs may remember how it was used to highlight the tragedy of battle in Peter Weir's moving World War I film *Gallipoli*.

The Classical Period (1750-1820)

To many people, 'classical' music is the opposite of popular music, the sort of music you are supposed to listen to with a serious demeanour and without gyrating or foot-tapping. The word 'classical', however, has another meaning and is applied to music composed in the second half of the 18th century and the first quarter of the 19th century. The Big Three composers of this period are Haydn, Mozart and Beethoven. Schubert is sometimes included, but others prefer to think of him as a Romantic – he probably had one foot in each camp.

In the Classical Period there is less emphasis on rhythm – it is not as strong, steady or consistent as it is in the Baroque Period. Melody is given a freer rein than formerly, even if the emotions are still held in check. In the Classical Period there were still basic conventions of form and structure with ideas being expressed within these confines.

One of the forms that really came into its own during the Classical Period is the symphony. Haydn is known as "the father of the symphony". His early ones were still short, three-movement entertainment pieces but after he had tossed off about 30 of these he added an extra movement and the symphonies became weightier without sacrificing any of their tunefulness. Mozart also wrote some entertainment-only symphonies, but the later ones were powerful works which paved the way for the monumental symphonies of Beethoven. With Haydn and Mozart it is easy to pick out a movement and enjoy it as a piece in its own right but the big symphonies of Beethoven have to be heard in toto and in sequence to have the full effect. They are so grand and magnificent that they frightened some 19th century composers away from symphonies entirely.

The sonata and concerto also developed greatly in the Classical Period, with Beethoven not outdoing Haydn or Mozart in tunefulness or entertainment value but coming up with works that were more complex and profound. The baroque sonata was for small ensembles while the classical sonata came to be for piano only or for solo instrument with piano either as accompaniment or, later, as equal partner. Beethoven was the king of the piano sonata, while Mozart was the undisputed master of the piano concerto. Chamber music developed greatly too, with composers beginning to write out separate parts for instruments in trios, quartets and other instrumental ensembles. The string trios and quartets of the Big Three are unsurpassed.

In baroque times opera had been used as a showcase for star singers, but the German Gluck set about trying to reform it. He wanted to make it a more cohesive art form with music and drama serving and complementing each other. He launched this in 1762 with *Orpheus and Eurydice* and must be credited with starting the music-drama style that has been the norm ever since. Shortly afterwards Mozart built on Gluck's beginnings and created both serious and comic masterpieces.

In the field of choral music, Bach and Handel remained supreme, though Haydn kept the oratorio fires burning, and he and Mozart wrote wonderful music in their masses. Beethoven, too, scored heavily with his 'Missa Solemnis'.

FRANZ JOSEPH HAYDN
(1732-1809)

Unlike some of the other musical geniuses, Haydn was a late developer. If he had died at the same age as Schubert (31) or Mozart (35), he would certainly not be in our Top 40 of composers. As it is, he is high on everyone's Top 10. He did not start writing symphonies until he was 27 and it was not until his 45th symphony, which he wrote in his 40th year, that the experts began applying the word "masterpiece". At that time Haydn was a musical man-of-all-work to the wealthy and cultured Count Esterhazy. For 30 years or so, he wrote, rehearsed and produced all the Esterhazy entertainments. He himself said:

> *My prince was content with all my works, I received approval. I could, as head of an orchestra, make experiments and run risks. I was set apart from the world, there was nobody in my vicinity to confuse and annoy me in my course and so I had to become original." During this Esterhazy period Haydn occasionally visited Vienna, where Mozart became his close friend and Beethoven was his pupil.*

Haydn's early life was spent in a small Austrian village where dancing on the green was a daily occurrence and where people sang folk songs for the sheer joy of it. This background undoubtedly had a great influence on the earthy peasant quality of Haydn's music, particularly in the symphonies and the chamber music. There are 104 symphonies and almost all have catchy tunes. Likewise, in the field of chamber music there are 83 string quartets, 67 string trios, 31 piano trios and much more. And what about sonatas? Fifty-two for piano alone – the man was unbelievable, a fountain of melody in almost every musical form. He was an opera composer as well and two oratorios – *The Creation* and *The Seasons* – are up there in the top bracket. That's still not all: there are concertos for trumpet, horn, cello and harpsichord that are universally popular. And what about the church music? *Stabat Mater* and a number of wonderful masses.

Haydn was not too fortunate in the marriage stakes. He made the error of marrying the older sister of the girl he loved. She turned out to be a shrew who gave him a very hard time.

This worked out well for us, however, because to avoid her company he would lock himself in his study and concentrate instead on the crotchets and the quavers.

In 1790 a non-music-loving Esterhazy succeeded to the princely throne. By then Haydn's music was famous all over Europe, so he decided to accept some of the invitations that were constantly showered on him. A man announcing himself as 'Salomon of London' invited him to England, where he was to compose new symphonies and conduct them in person. It turned out to be one of his most rewarding periods, both musically and financially. He composed two sets of 'London' or 'Salomon' symphonies, an even dozen (numbers 93 to 104). While in Britain Haydn received an honorary degree from Oxford University, reportedly fell in love with the wife of one of his hosts and took the opportunity to go to the races in Ireland.

Haydn spent the last six years of his life in Vienna where he held a kind of musical court in his lodgings, welcoming visiting admirers of every kind, from royalty to struggling artists. The French occupation of Vienna in 1809 shocked him immeasurably and he died the same year.

Haydn – A Middlebrow Mix

Symphony No. 45 (the 'Farewell')

Haydn's musicians were getting a little restless because the Prince was staying longer than usual at Esterhazy – they wanted to get back to their families in Vienna. Haydn was sympathetic and fashioned the last movement of this symphony in such a way that one by one the musicians blew their candles out and left the stage, leaving two violinists to finish the piece. We are told that the Prince took the hint and Haydn's little scheme served its purpose. The music itself is surprisingly dramatic for its time, with an urgency that persists throughout the first three movements. The finale opens with a very fast presto but as we proceed through the farewell sequence it becomes slower and slower until it finally comes to a full stop.

Symphony No. 94 (the 'Surprise')

Haydn was a man of good cheer and if you want cheerful music you need look no further than these symphonies. This one is a particularly good example – the minuet is a gem and the finale is Haydn at his happiest. There is also a little joke in the second movement which gives the symphony its nickname. The music is proceeding quietly and decorously, when suddenly there is a crashing chord from all available forces. Haydn said that he put that in "to make the ladies sit up". They still do.

Symphony No 96 (the 'Miracle')

This symphony got its name because, the story goes, a huge chandelier fell during the first performance in London. Miraculously no-one was injured because the enthusiastic audience had all pushed forward to get a better view of Mr Haydn, thus leaving a convenient empty space for the chandelier. The oboe plays a large part in the 'miracle' symphony – particularly in the slow second movement and with a folk-Austrian tune in the minuet movement. The finale is Haydn on top form with a little vivace that skips along delightfully.

Symphony No. 101 (the 'Clock')

Haydn had a great time in London – he was wined and dined and he really lapped it up. Far from dulling his creativity, the wine seemed to stimulate it. He produced glorious music during these few years in the 1790s. On hearing his 'Symphony No. 101', one critic was moved to write of "the inexhaustible, the wonderful, the sublime Haydn". The symphony gets its nickname from the second movement, the andante. Bassoon and plucked strings are heard throughout in what has been likened to the ticking of a clock. The tick-tock rhythm, however, does not obscure the beautiful melody.

Symphony No. 104 (the 'London')

The twelve last symphonies commissioned by the impresario Salomon are known as the 'Salomon' or 'London' symphonies, so there is no particular reason why this one should have been singled out as the 'London' symphony. It is very special, though, Haydn has been called "the father of the symphony" and the experts say that in emotional depth and power this one clearly foreshadows Beethoven. That doesn't mean that Haydn can't enjoy himself in the final movement, playing around with a catchy tune, 'Hot Cross Buns', that was popular in London at the time.

Trumpet Concerto

The trumpet has been around for a long time, but has developed a lot over the years. In ancient times it was straight and produced a very limited series of notes, like a bugle. Then trumpet-makers started to bend it, which made it more manageable, but it was only when valves were invented around 1800 that all the notes could be played and the trumpet became the sophisticated instrument it is today.

Attempts before the arrival of the valve trumpet to enlarge the number of notes available to the instrument led to the invention of various types of slide trumpet, which had a slide like a trombone, and of the keyed trumpet for which Haydn wrote this concerto. It was a man called Weidinger who invented the keyed trumpet. He was trumpet soloist of the Vienna Court Orchestra and had been experimenting for some years to improve the range of his instrument. Haydn immediately saw the possibilities of the new-fangled trumpet and wrote a concerto taking full advantage of its capabilities. Weidinger deserves much credit for effort, but apparently the extra notes and suppleness were achieved at the expense of tone. Haydn's work no doubt sounds a lot better today than when first performed in 1800. Haydn composed quite a few concertos but the 'Trumpet Concerto' was the last and the only one composed in his later years.

The first movement is festive and lively. It starts off quite conventionally with the trumpet doing nothing out of the ordinary, but it begins to really show off when it launches into its first solo. The second movement is a short, soulful andante, and the finale a brilliant rondo which really displays the virtuoso range of the solo trumpet and is one of the best known and most popular pieces of music ever written for the instrument.

String Quartet in G (the 'Emperor')

Haydn may not have invented the string quartet but he developed and perfected it. He wrote his first in 1750 at the age of 28, was captivated by the form and wrote another 82 in his lifetime. We don't hear many string quartets on *Music for Middlebrows*, but we have had this one because of the second movement. The theme is the Austrian national anthem, written at the request of the Kaiser, but it became notorious as *Deutschland Über Alles*. If you can forget the Third Reich connotations, in Haydn's hands it becomes simply a lovely piece of music.

WOLFGANG AMADEUS MOZART
(1756-1791)

To use an American expression, Mozart is "the Man". He must surely be the greatest musical genius of all time. Tchaikovsky called him the musical Christ, Haydn declared him to be the greatest composer known to him either in person or by name. I could go on and on quoting luminaries who put Mozart ahead of all others. Rossini, for instance, named Beethoven as the greatest but, when asked about Mozart, he said, "He is the *only*."

Mozart is certainly the only composer who wrote masterpieces in every musical form you can think of. He lived to be only 35 years of age, and one can only imagine what he might have accomplished had he reached the ripe old age of, say, 40.

A great deal has been written about Wolfgang Amadeus Mozart and his precocious talent, his exploitation by his father and, of course, his rivalry with the notorious Salieri. Not everything in the play and film *Amadeus* was far-fetched, however. Salieri was favoured by Emperor Josef far more than the spirited, irreverent youth and towards the end of his life, his mind wandering, Mozart did believe that Salieri was trying to poison him. No evidence against Salieri has ever been produced, though the older man must have been insanely jealous of the young Mozart.

Mozart was the prodigy of all prodigies (the runner-up is probably Mendelssohn). His father Leopold was a fine violinist in the Archbishop's orchestra in Salzburg and was also a music teacher. Under his guidance, Wolfgang began playing the piano at the age of four. At five he was able to compose little pieces of his own: his first symphony came at the age of eight, his first oratorio at eleven, his first opera at twelve. Leopold realised the marketability of his extraordinary son and he shepherded the boy and his talented sister Nannerl through Europe, making triumphal tours in Austria, Hungary, Belgium, France and England. Italy was the last port of call – by then Wolfgang had reached the advanced age of thirteen. He had performed all manner of musical party tricks for the nobility and royalty of Europe – he even proposed marriage to Queen Marie Antoinette of France, who smilingly suggested that he ask her again when he was older.

At the age of fifteen, Mozart was given a job by the Archbishop of Salzburg and he stayed there for ten years. Even as concertmaster he received little money and less respect. The Archbishop would not permit any travel or extra-curricular activities and, when Mozart rebelled, it was reported that he was actually propelled out of the room by a kick in the behind from his Eminence's steward.

After travelling for a while, Mozart settled in Vienna where he spent the last ten years of his life. He enjoyed a friendship with Haydn – in fact, it was more of a mutual admiration society – and, coincidentally, they both married a sister of the woman they fell in love with. Mozart fell for Aloysia Weber in Mannheim, but she favoured another and he settled for her sister Constanza. They were happy enough together, but Constanza's health was poor and she was no help to him as a household manager.

Mozart did not have to be sitting at a desk, quill in hand, to compose music. Tunes kept coming into his head wherever he was, even when indulging in one of his favourite pastimes, playing billiards. Some of his most fruitful hours were spent at the billiard table.

The Vienna years were extraordinarily productive. His four great operas were created here, the last seven and finest of his symphonies, the last seventeen piano concertos and myriad masterpieces of chamber music. Finally, there was the magnificent *Requiem*, commissioned by a mysterious black-clad stranger who appeared at Mozart's door. The ailing composer thought it might be an emissary from another world come to announce his approaching end – in fact it was the steward of a nobleman who hoped to pass the work off as his own. But in spite of this enormous output, the Mozarts were always in financial difficulties. There was a small stipend from the Emperor and the piano concertos were a money-spinner for a while, with a series of subscription concerts, but there was never enough. Ill health was inevitable and Mozart succumbed to it before he could finish the *Requiem*. Only a few people followed his coffin through a rainstorm to its unmarked pauper's grave. A contemporary musician (Salieri, perhaps?) is reported to have said:

> *It is a pity to lose so great a genius, but a good thing for us that he is dead. For if he had lived much longer, we should not have earned a crust of bread by our compositions.*

One point: most composers' works are identified by opus numbers, but Mozart's are given K numbers instead. K is short for Ludwig Köchel, a 19th century scholar who catalogued Mozart's works (as far as he could) in chronological order. To be accepted in the top musical circles you must use K numbers. It is not the done thing, for example, to say 'Piano Concerto No. 21' (though that is, it must be said, held to be preferable to asking for the 'Elvira Madigan'). If you can't remember that it's K467, you might get away with referring to it breezily as 'the C major'.

Mozart – A Middlebrow Mix

Symphonies Nos. 39 (K543), 40 (K550), 41 ('Jupiter' K551)

These three symphonic masterpieces were written in an astonishing burst of creativity during six weeks in the summer of 1788. It was almost as if Mozart were saying to himself, "I haven't got long to go, I have to get all these ideas and melodies down on paper while I can." He was in desperate straits at the time. His wife was ill and, deep in debt, he was reduced to sending frantic appeals to friends for an immediate loan. "God," he wrote in one of his appeals for money, "I am in a situation I would not wish on my worst enemy."

Symphony No. 39 was written when Mozart was at his lowest ebb but you would never guess this from the music, which is predominantly joyful and has a very popular minuet movement, which was one of the many classical pieces immortalised by a pop group – in this case, those well-known highbrows the Wombles. Of this trio of symphonies, Symphony No. 39 is by far the most light-hearted, with a lot of the wit and exuberance reminiscent of Papa Haydn.

Symphony No. 40 has come in for as much ecstatic praise as any piece of music ever written, including such tributes as:

> There are few things in art that are perfect; the G Minor symphony is one of them.

The work opens with a buoyant melody which became very famous some years ago when it featured in the pop charts under the title 'Mozart 40'. The second movement is tender with a heartfelt melancholy. The third movement is a more vigorous and dramatic minuet than is customary and its finale has a high-strung driving energy which lets up for a while to re-admit the melancholy and remind us of the composer's troubled state of mind.

Symphony No. 41 is known as 'Jupiter' and has earned that nickname by its grandeur and its extraordinary scope and power. It is all the more remarkable in that it was composed in about fourteen days. This, of course, does not mean that all the inspiration came to Mozart during that time. He himself explained:

> *I take out of my bag of memory what has previously been collected into it. For this reason, the committing to paper is done quickly enough.*

There are other Mozart symphonies that are lighter and more middlebrow, but those in the know tell us that 'Jupiter' is the greatest, the summit of the composer's creative work. The melodies are there, but they are cloaked in garments of imperial magnificence.

Three other symphonies by Mozart must be mentioned. The first is 'Symphony No. 35 in D' ('Haffner', K385). Mozart composed a number of works for the Haffner family of Salzburg. This one was to celebrate the elevation of Sigmund Haffner to the nobility. It was originally a serenade and has all the lightness and delicacy associated with that form. There is also the popular 'Haffner Serenade' (K250), composed for the wedding of Haffner's daughter. This one has a rondo for solo violin and orchestra which is popular in its own right. The other must-hear Mozart symphonies are 'No. 36 in C' (K425), bearing the nickname 'Linz' because it was composed in that city, and 'No. 38 in D' (K504), nicknamed 'Prague' because that was where it was first performed.

The Marriage of Figaro

The play by Beaumarchais on which this opera was based was banned in Vienna, so all was not plain sailing for Mozart when he had the idea of setting it to music. However, with the help of his librettist, Lorenzo da Ponte (who also collaborated on *Don Giovanni* and *Cosi Fan Tutte*) the obstacles were overcome. It wasn't an instant hit, though, when it was first performed in Vienna in 1786, but was a smash in Prague shortly afterwards.

The plot is so complicated that it defies summarising. There are love affairs, disguise and deceit involving Count Almaviva, who is tired of his wife Rosina and casts a roving eye. One of his targets is Susanna, fiancée of his valet Figaro and the Countess's maid. Then there is the amorous pageboy Cherubino (a mezzo-soprano role played by a woman) who gets into all sorts of hot water. Barbarina, the gardener's daughter and Marcellina, who turns out to be Figaro's mother, Dr Bartolo and Don Basilio all contribute to the shenanigans. My advice is not to strain yourself following the action, but to just wallow in the music, which has highlights galore: Figaro's 'Non piu andrai' ('Your days of philandering are over') warning Cherubino that a soldier's life is no bed of roses; the Countess's 'Porgi amor' regretting the loss of her husband's love and 'Dove sono', expressing her hope of regaining it, Cherubino's marvellous love song 'Voi che sapete' and Susanna's 'Deh vieni non tardar' rhapsodising about the coming joy of love.

Don Giovanni

A lot of people have written and composed about the legendary lecher Don Juan, but none with more genius than Mozart. *Don Giovanni* is an opera with a vast range of emotions and music that is by turn tragic, comic and heroic. It's set in Seville in the 17th century, and centres on the sexual exploits of the dastardly Don, assisted by his servant Leporello. The three women involved in the plot are Donna Anna, whose father (the Commandant) is killed by Don Giovanni and who swears vengeance with the help of her betrothed, Don Ottavio; Donna Elvira, abandoned by the Don but still holding a torch for him and the peasant girl Zerlina, who is about to be married to Masetto. Zerlina succumbs to the Don's charms, but is saved in the nick of time from becoming another notch on his gun. Don Giovanni gets his comeuppance in the end when a statue of the dead Commandant becomes an unwelcome dinner guest and delivers the unrepentant sinner to the demons of Hell.

Don Ottavio has one of the most celebrated of all tenor arias, 'Il mio tesoro' (the John McCormack recording is legendary for its extraordinary display of breath control); Leporello has the 'catalogue' aria in which he tells Donna Elvira of his master's 2,065 conquests; Don Giovanni has the wonderful serenade 'Deh vieni alla fenestra' with mandolin accompaniment and the duet 'La ci darem la mano' in which he exercises his technique on the susceptible Zerlina; Zerlina comforts Masetto in 'Vedrai carino' and the two Donnas also have their moments. This opera is just a treasure house of sublime music. It is easy to understand why many regard it as the greatest opera of all time. It is the operatic equivalent of Bach's 'Mass in B Minor' or Beethoven's 'Choral Symphony'.

The Magic Flute

Mozart sadly did not live to enjoy the success or the fruits of *The Magic Flute*. It had the most successful run of any of his operas – 197 performances in two years – but he died ten weeks after the première. Actually it was more of a pantomime than an opera. It's a huge fantasy with spoken dialogue, lots of show-stopping numbers and, in Papageno the birdcatcher, a virtuoso comic rôle.

Tamino sees a picture of Pamina, daughter of the evil Queen

of the Night, and falls in love with her. She is held captive in the
temple of the high priest, Sarastro, who turns out to be a good
guy and is holding her for her own protection. Tamino has to
prove himself worthy of her by undergoing some tough ordeals.
He comes through unscathed and wins the prize. He is aided
and abetted throughout by Papageno, who himself gets fixed
up with a suitable companion for life. Papageno has two
showstoppers: 'Ein Vogelfänger bin ich ja' ('I am a birdcatcher')
and 'Ein Mädchen oder weibchen' in which he longs for a female companion. Tamino has the tenor aria 'Dies Bildnis ist
bezaubernd schön' as he gazes bewitched at the picture of
Pamina, who herself has the lovely 'Ach ich fühl's' bemoaning
the fact that Tamino will not speak to her (this is one of the
ordeals he has to undergo). George Bernard Shaw said that the
music for Sarastro is the only music that could be put into the
mouth of God – outstanding is the hymn 'O Isis und Osiris'.

Horn Concerto No. 4 in F Flat (K495)

Mozart wrote the four horn concertos for a man called Leutgeb,
who had a cheese shop in Vienna and was sometimes carica-
tured – not least by Mozart himself – as a rough, simple sort of
fellow. However, when it came to blowing his horn he must
have been a man of great expertise and musical sensitivity, or
he couldn't have handled this music to Mozart's satisfaction.
The Rondo from the 'Concerto No. 4' is probably the most familiar piece of horn music in the entire repertoire. As Sir Thomas
Beecham wrote:

> *If I were dictator I should make it compulsory for every*
> *member of the population between the ages of four and eighty*
> *to listen to Mozart for at least a quarter of an hour daily.*

I don't know why he excluded the under-fours and the aged!

Flute Concerto No. 1 in G (K314) and Oboe Concerto in C

These concertos are the same, so you can make up your mind
whether you prefer the flute or the oboe. Mozart wrote the oboe
concerto first, but then he was commissioned by a Dutch amateur
flautist called de Jean to write some pieces for him. It seemed
that Mozart didn't much like the flute as an instrument, but he

needed the money (he always did!) and accepted the commission. Being pressed for time (he always was!) he decided to adapt the oboe concerto. All he had to do was change the key and do a bit of transposition in the copying. De Jean wasn't too pleased – in fact he didn't come up with the agreed money. There are wonderful tunes in these concertos – the finale is utterly irresistible on either instrument but I'm inclined to share Mozart's preference for the oboe.

Eine Kleine Nachtmusik (K525)

Mozart's light instrumental music comes under various titles, which are largely interchangeable. There is nothing really to distinguish a serenade from a divertimento and 'notturno', which he also used, is a nocturnal serenade. A good number of these pieces were commissioned by wealthy families for special occasions and their individual characteristics were determined in the main by the occasion. The fact that many were intended to be played in the open air accounts, for example, for the important part played by the wind instruments. 'Eine Kleine Nachtmusik' was originally written for string quartet, but is now more often heard played by full string orchestra. It is probably the most played of any Mozart piece, the reason being that the tunes are some of the most delightful and memorable that Mozart ever wrote.

Piano Concerto No. 21 in C (K467)

It was been suggested that the reason Mozart was able to write so many wonderful piano concertos was simply because he was a brilliant operatic composer. The piano concertos are full of the quick changes of situation, the brisk interplay of characters that one can find in his operas and are handled with the same mastery. Thus their immediate appeal and popularity. There must be more to it than that, but it is certainly true that a lot of the great tunes in the piano concertos could have jumped right out of *The Magic Flute*. The renowned musicologist Alfred Einstein ranked the piano concertos as the peak of Mozart's achievement in the orchestral domain. He expressed the view that if only the Viennese public had paid greater attention to the composer than it did, we might well have had ten or twelve masterpieces in the last four or five years of Mozart's life, rather than only two, adding that he wrote no more piano concertos once he had no opportunity to play them.

The years 1784-86 were among the happiest in Mozart's life. He was living in Vienna and was happy in his recent marriage. His opera *Il Seraglio* was proving successful at various theatres and he was enjoying recognition as a piano virtuoso. It was during these few years that he composed the majority of his great piano concertos. One of them was 'No. 21 in C', which was first heard in 1785 with the composer as soloist. This concerto, of course, has attained great heights of popularity since the andante was used as theme music for the film *Elvira Madigan*. The piece opens with a march-like theme which dominates the first movement. Then comes the celebrated andante – one of Mozart's most ethereal creations – with the piano weaving a spell to the accompaniment of muted violins. The concerto concludes with a light-hearted romp of a finale, full of operatic gaiety.

Clarinet Concerto in A (K622)

The clarinet is a member of the woodwind family – the other principal members being the oboe, flute and bassoon. The term woodwind comes from the fact that most of the original instruments were made from wood. In this age of technology, however, many of the instruments are made of metal and indeed other, more valuable, materials. James Galway, for example, is sometimes known as "the man with the golden flute". There are many different types of clarinet which vary greatly in range and pitch, but the two most common and standard members of the symphony orchestra are the B-flat and the A.

The clarinet is the most versatile of the woodwind instruments. It can produce a velvety or strident tone as required and in military bands it takes the place of the violins. The first mention of the clarinet being used in orchestras occurs around 1740, but it was really with the works composed by Mozart for his friend Anton Stadler that the clarinet came to be accepted as a solo instrument capable of great virtuosity and lyricism. Mozart developed the capacities of the clarinet to a very high degree and three of his works are still amongst the most popular in the clarinet repertoire – the 'Concerto in A' (K622), the 'Quintet in A for clarinet and strings' (K581) and the 'Trio in E Flat for clarinet, viola and piano' (K498). Mozart also features the clarinet in many of his symphonies, much more than Haydn or any other composer of the time did and a close relative of the clarinet, the basset horn, plays a leading role in some of his operas.

The clarinet was, however, very much in its infant stages when Mozart composed his concerto in 1790 and Stadler must have been something of a genius to have been able to handle its intricacies. It seems that Stadler owed Mozart money at the time of the composer's death, and was also responsible for the loss of some of the composer's manuscripts, so he must indeed have had some special qualities. The first movement is multi-faceted, combining symphonic brilliance, operatic lyricism and solo virtuosity. The second movement, the adagio, stresses the singing qualities of the solo instrument against a rich orchestral background and is one of Mozart's most sublime creations. The finale is a hunting rondo with some wistfulness lurking beneath the surface gaiety.

Violin Concerto in G (K216)

As a performer, Mozart is more often thought of as a keyboard player than as a violinist but his father Leopold wrote to him once:

> *You yourself have no idea how well you play the violin. If only you would do yourself justice and play with boldness and spirit and fire, as if you were the first violinist in Europe.*

Leopold knew what he was talking about. He was a fine violinist himself and the author of a textbook on the art of violin playing which was regarded as the most important of the day.

Mozart's entire output for solo violin and orchestra was written between the ages of seventeen and twenty. This includes the five major violin concertos, four of which were composed in 1775 when he was concert master at the court of the Archbishop of Salzburg. Mozart composed the concertos as part of his duties at the court and originally played the solo parts himself, but they were probably also played before long by his successor, Antonio Brunetti.

It is a toss-up as to whether the most popular of Mozart's violin concertos is 'No. 3' or 'No. 5' – sorry, I should say the 'G

Minor' (K216) or the 'A Major' (K219). My personal preference is marginally for the 'G Major', which opens with a cheery march from Mozart's own musical play *Il Re Pastore*, completed early that same year. Then follows the most sublime adagio of all, once described as having fallen straight from Heaven and the concerto concludes with a folkish rondo.

Other Mozart Must-Hears

Of the lighter orchestral works mention must be made of the 'Six German Dances' (K600). Another set of 'German Dances' (K605) has the famous 'Sleigh Ride'. Of all the piano Sonatas the best known is 'No. 11' (K331), because it has the celebrated 'Rondo alla turca' which is often played on its own and in various arrangements. There are over 200 chamber works, including the most magnificent quartets and quintets. If you have a few years to spare you should make their acquaintance.

LUDWIG VAN BEETHOVEN
(1770-1827)

It has been said that Beethoven, more than any other composer, deserves to be called the Shakespeare of music, for he reaches to the heights and plumbs the depths of the human spirit as no other composer has done. The French composer Georges Bizet placed him on the same plane as Dante, Michelangelo, Shakespeare, Homer and Moses, and called him "the Titan...the Prometheus of music".

Beethoven, however, had humble beginnings. He was born in Bonn and his early life was a struggle as there was never any money in the family. He started piano lessons when he was four and was kept at it by a tyrannical, alcoholic and sometimes violent father. He managed to visit Vienna, however, when he was seventeen and when the young Beethoven met Mozart, the great Wolfgang is reputed to have said:

Watch this young man, he will yet make a noise in the world.

Five years later, after his father's death, Ludwig went back to live in Vienna. He took lessons in composition from Haydn, and soon began to make a name for himself. By all accounts, however, he was an unpleasant sort of fellow (not in the same league as Wagner, who was a monster) but bad mannered and thoroughly disagreeable. Beethoven, of course, had a great deal to contend with. He was barely 30 when the first symptoms of deafness appeared and he wrote: "I must confess that I am living a miserable life." His condition rapidly deteriorated, yet during the years 1800 to 1815, before he became totally deaf, eight of his nine symphonies were completed, as well as five piano concertos, the opera *Fidelio*, the violin concertos, the Razumovsky string quartets, the great piano sonatas and sonatas for violin and piano. What did he have left to compose? Well! More quartets and sonatas, the 'Missa Solemnis', and his most monumental work - the 9th or 'Choral' symphony.

Volumes have been written about Beethoven's mysterious letters to his 'Immortal Beloved', but her identity has never been established. Beethoven remained a bachelor, but his brother Caspar did him no favours when he left Ludwig in charge of his only son Karl. Beethoven took the guardianship very seriously, but his nephew was a ne'er-do-well who gave him no peace for eleven years and was finally banished in disgrace from Vienna in 1826.

In 1827 Beethoven caught pneumonia and died, but a post-mortem revealed that he had been suffering from many internal disorders. One would like to give credence to this contemporary report:

> *On March 26 the Viennese heavens were split with lightning and growled with thunder. It was almost as if the city were giving voice to grief. A peal of thunder rumbled in Beethoven's deathroom. Ever the rebel, Beethoven raised a defiant fist toward the heavens. Then he fell back and died.*

Beethoven – A Middlebrow Mix

Symphony No. 5

I first heard Beethoven's 'Symphony No. 5' at the Savoy Cinema in Limerick around 1950, where it was played by what was then the Radio Éireann Symphony Orchestra. I was at Glenstal Priory (now Abbey) at the time and before going to the concert we had sessions with Dom Paul McDonald so that we were familiar with all the main themes of the symphony.

I suppose that the 'Fifth' would be at the top of everyone's list of popular symphonies. It is invoked even more often than the Fifth Amendment. It is not necessarily everybody's favourite, but is certainly the most familiar. The instant we hear that celebrated four-note opening, we know exactly where we are. The opening itself has been likened to the sound of fate knocking at the door and some analysts have suggested that the symphony is a musical representation of Beethoven's struggle with and final victory over the adverse forces of fate. The years around the turn of the 18th century were very difficult for Beethoven. He had to contend with a disastrous deterioration in his hearing, by the time he had completed this masterpiece, he was totally deaf. The opening rhythm corresponds to the V-sign (dot dot dot dash) in Morse code and became even more widely known during World War II, when the Allies broadcast it on the radio as a victory signal.

> *In the first movement, Beethoven builds a dramatic and monumental structure on the 'famous four' notes. In contrast, the second movement is calm and easy-flowing, in the form of a funeral march. The third movement is a scherzo, but not literally, as there is nothing 'jokey' about it. Then comes the famous bridge, which keeps us in suspense as to whether we will be plunged into despondency or soar to the heights of victory. Celebrations are in order as the finale turns out to be joyous and triumphant.*

Piano Concerto No. 5 (the 'Emperor')

Beethoven composed the major part of his fifth piano concerto in 1809 under conditions which were anything but conducive to creative work. In May of that year the French army, under

Napoleon, marched on Vienna and opened siege During the bombardment, we are told, Beethoven crouched in a cellar holding a pillow over his head to spare his ears the pain. Following a severe battering, Vienna capitulated and the French moved in to begin a short but oppressive occupation. It was during this time that Beethoven worked on the concerto which was first performed in Leipzig two years later. According to a contemporary review:

> *The crowded audience was put into a state of enthusiasm...this is without doubt one of the most original, imaginative and effective of all existing concertos.*

The title was not given to it by Beethoven himself, who wasn't at all well disposed towards Napoleon at the time. We are told that during the piece's first Vienna performance, before an audience containing many officers of the conquering French armies, one of the Napoleonic old guard leapt to his feet and cried, 'C'est l'Empereur!', thus naming the concerto. It's much more likely, though, that the name came from the English publisher J B Cramer, who happened to refer to the work as "an emperor among concertos". This is the only concerto in which Beethoven himself was not the soloist for its first performance. At that time, in 1812, he had ceased to appear as a concert pianist, owing to the drastic deterioration in his hearing.

The opening of the concerto is unusual – there are three imposing chords from the orchestra, separated by brief forays on the piano. For some time after this the orchestra occupies itself with a mighty introduction. It finally yields the spotlight to the piano and the movement really gets into its stride. It's a very long opening movement – as long as some of Mozart's complete concertos. The second movement is subdued and solemn, with the piano presenting a lovely gentle melody and the finale is a full-blooded rondo with piano and orchestra making the most of a catchy main tune and showing all the imperial grandeur of its title.

Violin Concerto in D

It's interesting, I think, that almost all the great violin concertos have been the sole work in that form by their composers. One can think of Brahms, Tchaikovsky, Dvorak, Sibelius, Beethoven – all of whom composed only one violin concerto. This can be explained perhaps by the fact that most composers play the piano while few are practising violinists. In composing, they have usually relied on the practical advice of some virtuoso. Beethoven, however, was an accomplished string player. He began studying violin and viola when he was only eight and by 1778 he had acquired sufficient technique to be given a position as violinist in the Bonn court chapel and theatre.

The soloist in the first performance of the 'Violin Concerto in D' was Franz Clement, an eminent virtuoso of the day. He played it at a public concert in 1806 but without a great deal of success. The fault was probably more Beethoven's than Clement's – the composer delivered the manuscript at the last minute and Clement had virtually to read the solo part at sight. However, he himself did not contribute to the seriousness of the occasion. He was something of a musical clown and between the first and second movements he decided to stick in as a diversion a piece of his own, played on one string and with the violin held upside down.

The concerto opens in pensive mood, the main theme being ushered in by four raps on the kettledrum, said to have been suggested by a neighbour's knocks on the door when the composer was at work late one night. One critic didn't take too kindly to the kettledrum and sneeringly referred to the piece as the "kettledrum concerto". However, in spite of its inauspicious beginning, the work went on to be recognised as one of the most beautiful of all the violin concertos. Unlike many others it was not conceived as a confrontation between the soloist and the orchestra, and it does not have the devilishly difficult passages designed to dazzle the audience and display the soloist's virtuosity. The violin, particularly in the first and second movements, is given ample opportunity to do what it does best – to sing – in passages with solo parts integrated into the overall orchestral fabric. You probably won't even notice that the opening taps on the timpani are subtly repeated throughout the long first movement. The second movement is a soulful meditation, with the soloist's cadenza leading us into the bright rondo finale.

Piano Sonata No. 14 (the 'Moonlight')

Beethoven was born just about the time that the pianoforte came into general use, superseding the harpsichord. In very simple terms, the difference was that it was now possible to play louder or softer on the piano by striking the keys more or less forcefully, an effect not possible on the harpsichord. Beethoven took full advantage of this new instrument and he was constantly pushing its capacities. He continued to do this even when he could no longer hear the results and was no longer able to be the virtuoso interpreter of his own works. The piano was Beethoven's instrument and his concertos and sonatas have a strength and passion that are unparalleled.

Of all the sonatas, the one that has captured the imagination of the public is the so-called 'Moonlight'. This title was bestowed on the piece by a poet called Rellstat, who said that the shimmering serenity of the first movement suggested Lake Lucerne in the moonlight. Beethoven dedicated the sonata, composed in 1801, to a former pupil, Countess Giulietta Guicciardi, who was then seventeen and about half the age of the love-smitten composer.

Beethoven was being innovative and experimental in opening his sonata with the slow movement. It's really more of a prelude, with the movements that follow putting the virtuosic skills of any performer to the test.

Symphony No. 3 (the 'Eroica')

Beethoven first dedicated this symphony to Napoleon Bonaparte, but when he heard that Napoleon had declared himself Emperor, he tore up the title page in a fit of rage. On a fresh page he wrote the words: "Heroic Symphony – composed to celebrate the memory of a great man." I would particularly recommend to middlebrows the third movement – the scherzo – with memorable moments for French horns.

Symphony No. 6 (the 'Pastoral')

The 'Pastoral' was directly inspired by nature. Each of this great work's five movements was given a subtitle by the composer, who said that they express the emotions aroused by country scenes. The movements are subtitled as follows: first, 'Serene impressions awakened by arrival in the country'; second, 'By the brook'; third, 'A merry gathering of country folk'; fourth, 'The tempest'; fifth, 'Shepherd's song, glad and thankful feelings after the storm'. The titles reflect the mood of each movement, but it's worth drawing attention to the recognisable birdsong in the second movement, which has a celebrated melody voiced by the oboe. The third movement is a sort of German hoedown and then in the fourth movement we have the fury of the storm, with lots of timpani that, on abatement, brings us back to a lovely gentle melody that brings peace to the soul.

Symphony No. 9 (the 'Choral')

This mammoth work is the pinnacle of Beethoven's achievement. The composer himself was nominally the conductor at the first performance in Vienna in 1824. The poor man was stone deaf and continued to wave his arms when the music was over. One of the soloists gently turned him around to receive the audience's ovations. The fourth movement is the celebrated setting of Schiller's 'Ode to Joy' for soloists, chorus and orchestra. Beethoven had been preparing this symphony for many years, making notes and sketches. Though there is wonderful music in the first three movements, anyone who knows this symphony is aware that it is all a build-up to the incredible outpouring of joy in the concluding movement where Beethoven gives voice to his ideal of universal brotherhood. After the collapse of the Berlin Wall, this was the piece chosen to celebrate that historic and symbolic occasion, and the world's greatest orchestras came together to perform it on the site of the Wall itself. The resulting recording, conducted by Leonard Bernstein, is available under the title 'Ode to Freedom' and I can recommend it without reservation.

Egmont Overture

Beethoven wrote a number of pieces to order for a performance of Goethe's tragedy *Egmont* at the Vienna court theatre. The story of the play tells of the revolt of the people of the Netherlands against the oppressive rule of Spain. Egmont is the hero, though he himself dies. The overture is a fine work and a good example of Beethoven's style at its most heroic.

Leonore Overture No. 3

Beethoven preferred the title *Leonore* for his only opera, now generally known as *Fidelio*. Leonore is the heroine, but assumes the name Fidelio when she disguises herself as a man. The first three overtures written for the opera are still known as 'Leonore', however. They were considered too symphonic for the stage, and Beethoven eventually came up with a 'Fidelio' overture, a shorter piece which is a suitable prelude to the action.

'Leonore No. 3' is now usually played between the dungeon scene and the finale (though not everybody agrees that it should appear here). It is a mighty symphonic poem which sums up the heroic issues of the opera and it's hard for anything that follows not to be something of an anti-climax. It's very effective in the concert hall, with the famous trumpet call coming from offstage or someplace unexpected in the auditorium.

Für Elise

A delightful bagatelle known to all amateur pianists, this piece was written as a birthday present for a girl called Therese, but Beethoven's handwriting wasn't up to much and the printer assumed it was Elise.

Sonata No. 5 in F (the 'Spring')

If you like the combination of violin and piano, don't miss this happy, melodic work. It is the most popular of all Beethoven's sonatas – the other very famous one being 'No. 9 in A' (the 'Kreutzer').

FRANZ SCHUBERT
(1797-1828)

Many of the great composers died young, but Schubert was given less time than any – only 31 years. Had he lived longer he would certainly be classed as a Romantic rather than being half-and-half.

Franz was one of thirteen children of a village schoolmaster. Thanks to a scholarship he was able to enter the Imperial Court Choir School in Vienna at the age of eleven and, while a chorister, studied piano, violin and harmony with the notorious Salieri as his teacher of composition. When he was sixteen he taught for a while in his father's school, but he wasn't cut out to be a teacher and gave it up after a few years to devote himself completely to music.

Schubert always had the ambition to compose successful operas but he never made it in this field. However, he became the master songwriter instead and this is where his passion lay. He was very industrious and wrote with great fluency, once writing 150 songs in a single year. Franz Liszt called him "the most poetic of them all". He had an extremely lyrical gift and melody flowed from him in an unending stream. It was said that he could compose the music for a song in the time it would take to read the words. He could also produce piano pieces and chamber works suitable for drawing-room performance. These brought him an income which, if meagre, was at least regular. He could also count on friends to help him out when he needed them. Schubert had a great talent for friendship and loved to spend time with poets, artists, actors and fellow composers. He would meet them in the late afternoon and evening, having spent the earlier part of the day (usually from six o'clock in the morning) working at his desk. Many of Schubert's works were first heard at gatherings in small private houses which came to be known as 'Schubertiades'.

Schubert's last five years of life were marred by ill health. It seems that he contracted syphilis and was in and out of hospital, sometimes for weeks at a time. Then, at the age of 31, an attack of typhus put an end to him. On his tombstone, placed as close as possible to that of his idol Beethoven, was inscribed:

Music has buried here a rich treasure but still fairer hopes.

It was not until ten years after his death that much attention was paid to Schubert's music. Schumann, who had spent the night in tears on hearing of Schubert's death, found in Vienna pieces till then unknown and Mendelssohn performed them. He did the same for Bach 80 years after Johann Sebastian's death. Had he not lived so close to Haydn, Mozart and Beethoven, Schubert might have been sooner recognised, but during his lifetime his genius was overshadowed by theirs. He himself had said, "My music is the production of my genius and my misery."

Incidentally, as Mozart had his Köchel who gave all his works K numbers, Schubert had his Deutsch, a 20th century scholar who catalogued the works and gave them D numbers.

Schubert – A Middlebrow Mix

Symphony No. 8 in B Minor (the 'Unfinished')

In 1822 Schubert was elected an honorary member of a music society in Graz and as a mark of gratitude said he would send them the score of a new symphony. A year later, when reminded of his promise, he sent the society the score of what is now known as the 'Unfinished Symphony'. It seems that the director of the society held on to the score for 42 years before mentioning it to anyone. By then Schubert was long gone – and in fact he had made no effort to complete the symphony even though he lived another six years after submitting the two movements to the society. He must have felt that he had said all he had to say in this particular work and that there was no point in continuing. As it is, it is a profound masterpiece and was destined to rise to great heights of popular favour. The first movement has one of the best known and best loved melodies in all symphonic music. The second movement starts off with another wonderful flowing melody given out by French horns, bassoons and strings. Then we get a second theme, tender and lovely. Things become more dramatic for a while but the original mood returns for the symphony to end in peaceful serenity.

In 1928, in an effort to commemorate the centenary of Schubert's death, an American record company offered a prize of $10,000 to the composer who could do the best job of finishing the symphony. The idea was treated with the scorn it deserved.

Quintet in A (the 'Trout') for Piano and Strings

Of all the chamber works of Franz Schubert, the best known by far is the 'Quintet in A'. Indeed, it has become one of the most frequently performed pieces in the entire chamber music repertoire, though it was not published during the composer's lifetime.

In 1819 Schubert was enjoying a summer vacation with some friends in the town of Steyr in Upper Austria. Musical evenings were spent at the home of Sylvester Paumgartner, an amateur cellist who commissioned the quintet, stipulating its instrumentation and that it should contain a set of variations on Schubert's song 'Die Forelle' (the 'Trout') which had been written in 1817. The combination of instruments is unusual, with piano and double bass joining a string trio.

There are five movements, which is also unusual – most chamber compositions of the classical era have three or four. All five are wonderful, but it is the fourth that gives the pieces its enormous popularity. This is marked Andantino, but usually referred to as the 'Theme and Variations'. The theme is established by the violin, accompanied only by the other strings. It is then taken up in turn by piano, cello and double bass. In this movement's fifth variation there is an exquisite cello solo and finally the piano launches into the wonderful rippling accompaniment so familiar from the song. Don't stop there, though – make sure you stay for the quintet's finale, an energetic movement in the Hungarian style, full of boisterous high spirits.

Piano Music

Robert Schumann once said that:

> *As a composer for the piano Schubert stands alone (in some respects even above Beethoven) in that his writing is more pianistic, that is to say the piano's full resources are effectively brought into play.*

There are 21 piano sonatas, and the great 'Wanderer Fantasy'. This is a set of variations that get its name from one of Schubert's songs. Schumann said of it that, "Schubert would like, in this work, to condense the whole orchestra into two hands". Liszt later arranged it for piano and orchestra, turning it into a sort of piano concerto. The following pieces are middlebrow musts.

Impromptu No. 4 (D899)

There are two sets of four impromptus and this one, from the second set, is the most popular. A gorgeous tune in the left hand is embellished with cascading right-hand arpeggios.

Moment Musical No. 3 in F Minor

This is the most famous of the 'musical moments' – D780 – but you should listen to all six. They are little lyrical masterpieces.

Marche Militaire No. 1

There are three military marches but this is the one we all know – often heard now in its orchestral version. Stravinsky borrowed it for his tongue-in-cheek 'Circus Polka', written to accompany a parade of elephants – check it out, it's great fun!

Rosamunde – Incidental Music

Schubert wrote incidental music for a play called *Rosamunde, Princess of Cyprus*. The play, by all accounts, was a disaster and unfortunately Schubert's music sank with it until many years later it was discovered in a cellar in Vienna by Arthur Sullivan (of Gilbert and Sullivan fame) and George Grove, the man responsible for the exhaustive musical dictionary that bears his name. It is reported that in sheer delight they jumped around in excitement, leap-frogging around the room. The highlights of this wonderful incidental music are two graceful and tuneful ballet sequences and a happy overture which was previously used by Schubert as a prelude to the opera *The Magic Harp*.

Songs

Schubert is credited with bringing the German art-song – or Lied – to its highest point of perfection. A Lied is more than a musical setting of a poem. It differs from an ordinary song in that the piano is more than just an accompaniment. It is a full partner, as in, for instance, sonatas for piano and violin. The piano plays as important a part as the voice in evoking the atmosphere of the poem. Even though each Lied is an artwork in itself, composers began grouping them into sets called 'song-cycles' that told a story or treated a theme (often unrequited love) throughout. To achieve their full effect, song-cycles should be heard in toto, but they are often very long so you would need to set aside a good half-hour or more to savour 'Die Schöne Müllerin' ('The Fair Maid of the Mill') or 'Die Winterreise' ('Winter Journey').

In the meantime, some of the most popular individual songs are: 'Ave Maria', which ties with Gounod's as the most popular hymn to the Virgin. In 1825 Schubert referred to his 'Ave Maria' in a letter to his father in which he spoke of a musical evening:

> *My new song from Walter Scott's* Lady of the Lake *especially had much success. They also wondered greatly at my piety, which I expressed in a hymn to the Holy Virgin.*

'Die Forelle (the 'Trout') has a delicious rippling accompaniment and achieved further fame in the great Quintet; 'Der Erlkönig' ('The Erl King') is a setting of Goethe's tragic poem in which a father, with his sick child on horseback, tries to outride Death. Other great songs include 'Ständchen' ('Serenade') and 'Gretchen am Spinnrade' ('Gretchen at the Spinning Wheel'), as well as 'An Die Musik' ('To Music'), 'Wer ist Sylvia' ('Who is Sylvia') and 'Heidenröslein' ('Little Rose on the Heath').

OTHER CLASSICAL NOTEWORTHIES

Christoph von Gluck
(1714-1787)

The first production of Gluck's opera *Orpheus and Eurydice* took place in Vienna at the court of the Empress Maria Theresa. There were some adverse comments at the first performance in 1762, but the Empress liked the opera and after the third performance presented Gluck with a snuffbox filled with ducats. The success of the later Paris production was so great that Gluck's former pupil, Marie Antoinette, granted him a pension - he seems to have had a way with royal ladies.

The success of *Orpheus and Eurydice* came after many years of travelling and producing new operas throughout Europe. He also gave cello recitals and a famous concert in London in 1746 on "musical glasses". I think the advertisement for this concert is worth quoting:

> *A Concerto upon Twenty-Six Drinking Glasses, tuned with Spring-Water, accompanied with the Whole Band, being a new instrument of his own invention; upon which he performs whatever may be done on a Violin or Harpsichord and thereby hopes to Satisfy the Curious, as well as Lovers of Musick.*

There was more than one spurious claim here – he wasn't the first to make music on glasses (an Irishman called Puckeridge had preceded him) and as for being able to perform "whatever may be done on a Violin or Harpsichord" – some chance!

The story of *Orpheus and Eurydice* has been a favourite of opera composers (Monteverdi and Offenbach were others who treated it). In the Greek legend Orpheus, the 'inventor of music', goes off to the Underworld to retrieve his beloved wife. Pluto, ruler of the Underworld, agrees to release Eurydice as long as Orpheus does not turn around and look at her on the way out. He cannot resist and loses her forever. Gluck however, was a softie, and gave his opera a happy ending, with Eurydice being restored to life by the God of Love.

In the early days the part of Orpheus was sung by a castrato (a man who had been castrated in order to preserve his youthful soprano or alto voice). Nowadays the part is usually taken by a woman. The most celebrated aria is 'Che faro senza Euridice?' ('What shall I do without Eurydice?') and there is also the sublime 'Dance of the Blessed Spirits' with a famous flute solo (also arranged for violin by Kreisler). This describes the bliss of the spirits in the delectable fields of Elysium. Orpheus also describes this beautiful place in the aria 'Che puro ciel', which is enhanced by a lovely oboe obbligato.

Luigi Boccherini
(1743-1805)

The Italian Boccherini spent a lot of time in Spain. On his first visit there in 1769 he was patronised by the King's brother and later by Charles IV himself. He composed a great variety of music – operas, symphonies, much chamber music – but he is principally remembered for a little minuet which must have charmed the ladies of the Spanish Court. It comes from 'String Quartet, Opus 14, No. 5' (one of the 170 quartets he composed) and as if it wasn't already well known, it achieved greater notoriety in the film *The Ladykillers*, when 'played' by Alec Guinness and his group of criminals masquerading as chamber musicians.

The Romantic Period (1820-1910)

To prevent the Romantic Period becoming top heavy, I have divided it into three sections: early, middle and late. This is problematic, though, because some composers lived very short lives while others lived for ages. Some were precocious geniuses, while others were late starters. To save myself headaches, I have divided them mainly by date of birth.

In the 19th century the expression of emotion became all important. No longer did composers consider it necessary to stick to strict forms. They did sometimes use the established ones (sonata, symphony, concerto) but adapted and expanded them and, if it suited their purposes, invented new ones. The Romantic Period was one of individual expression. The music became an uninhibited outpouring of joy and sorrow, tenderness, passion, despair, ecstasy, exuberance – all the feelings of which the human soul is capable. Some composers were able to express themselves in the four-movement symphony (Mendelssohn, Tchaikovsky); others had to create new vehicles to suit their emotional needs (Liszt's tone poems, Berlioz's dramatic symphony, Wagner's music-dramas). Then there were some who preferred to express themselves in shorter forms – songs and piano pieces became a major part of the output of many composers. There are far more middlebrow composers in this period than in any other, because melody reigned supreme. There may be one or two exceptions (aren't there always?) but generally the Romantics were composers of lyrical, sensuous, expansive melodies that are immediately appealing.

Rhythm was not a priority with the early Romantics (Chopin's waltzes were not intended for ballroom dancing), but in the middle period it came into its own again with the incorporation of strong folk rhythms into compositions. Most of the 'nationalist' composers – those that wanted to express the character of their native land by the use of folk songs and rhythms – are in the middle. Examples that spring to mind are Smetana of The Czech Republic, Borodin of Russia and Grieg of Norway.

The 19th century too was the era of huge expansion in the size of orchestras and ideas about orchestration. Berlioz was the trend-setter. He thought an ideal orchestra should have 121 players and, for special occasions, 465. The Romantics experimented with instruments which became capable of a much greater variety of sound (valves made a huge difference to wind instruments). They also became fascinated with tone colour and produced rich, rare and variegated orchestral sounds. Liszt and Wagner took up where Berlioz left off and other mighty orchestrators were Dvorak, Tchaikovsky, Rimsky-Korsakov and Mahler.

Music reached a much wider audience in the Romantic Period. Previously it had been somewhat elitist and supported by royal, aristocratic, ecclesiastical or, at least, wealthy patrons who, naturally, expected a say in what the composers produced. If you failed to produce the sort of music your patron required, you could be out on the street. In the 19th century, however, concert-going gradually became much more popular. The audiences became the patrons and expected fresh and innovative works. Virtuoso performers like Liszt and Paganini were the pop stars of the day. Publishing, too, came into its own and publications, particularly of songs and piano pieces for home consumption, became a money-making business.

Let's get on with talking about the composers themselves – but not before mentioning opera. Wagner was a law unto himself, but this was the Golden Age of Italian opera - Rossini, Donizetti, Bellini, Puccini, Verdi: you'll hear about them all as you read on.

THE EARLY-ROMANTICS (1820-1850)

CARL MARIA VON WEBER
(1786-1826)

Carl Maria von Weber could just as easily have been included with the classicists and only just got into the Top 40. There were a few other contenders but, apart from the operas, Weber has some lovely instrumental pieces to his credit. His father hoped to exploit him as a prodigy as Leopold Mozart had with his son – something Papa Weber knew all about as he was related to the Mozarts by marriage.

Carl Maria was not a healthy boy, but he was forced to practise the piano and violin for hours on end and toured with his parents' troupe of strolling players. His father was a violinist, his mother an actress and her death broke up the family troupe. It was then that Carl Maria, not yet in his teens, began serious music studies with Haydn's younger brother Michael. He had written two operas by the time he was thirteen. The second was performed but failed, as did a third. Nevertheless, Weber continued his studies in Vienna and became a remarkable pianist and an excellent conductor. His first job conducting the Breslau Opera was a failure, but in 1813 he became director of the Prague Opera, and that was a much greater success. Three years later he moved to the Dresden Court Theatre for what was to become a lifelong appointment.

In spite of his disciplinarian father, Weber was an easygoing youth with an apparent talent for getting into hot water. On one occasion he had to leave Stuttgart because, while in the employ of the Duke of Württenberg, some funds entrusted to his keeping disappeared. He also lost a good singing voice by accidentally drinking nitric acid and was nearly ruined through a liaison with an unscrupulous prima donna. His marriage to Caroline Brandt, who loved and understood him, settled him down and created the ambience for serious work.

In Germany, as elsewhere, Italian opera was all the rage, and Weber dedicated himself to creating an opera that would be German in every way. It took him three years to write *Der Freischütz*, but it was a landmark, the first truly German Romantic opera. It was based on an old German legend and its character was powerfully German in both drama and music. With this work Weber paved the way for Wagner, introducing the leitmotif (a theme associated with a particular character or circumstance) and used the orchestra more than anyone before him to create atmosphere and heighten dramatic effect. Wagner at least had the good grace to acknowledge his debt to his predecessor.

Der Freischütz was by far the most popular German opera of the first half of the 19th century, and was translated into numerous languages. The follow-ups *Euryanthe* and *Oberon* were not as successful but Weber had accomplished his mission. He had always been frail and succumbed to tuberculosis at the age of 39.

Weber – A Middlebrow Mix

Der Freischütz (the 'Free-Shooter')

Weber took quite a while to compose this opera – he worked at it intermittently over a period of three years – and *Der Freischütz* finally reached the stage of the Berlin Opera House on 18 June 1821. The patriotic Germans were very anxious for the opera to succeed. At that time the ruling spirit in operatic matters in Berlin was a Franco-Italian called Spontini and the nationalists regarded Weber as the one person capable of dethroning him. Well! June 18, the date of the Battle of Waterloo, proved to be as great a day for Weber as it had been for Wellington. The applause from an overflowing house was such as had never been heard before, in Germany at any rate. That this magnificent homage was not merely the outcome of party spirit has been amply proved by the enduring success of the opera.

The plot is based on the legend of 'magic bullets' which never miss their mark and which can be obtained through a pact with the spirits of hell. The demon Samiel has the hunter Caspar in his power. Caspar's only way out is to find a substitute and he sets his sights on the young Max, who is in love with Agatha. In the end Caspar gets his comeuppance, the young lovers find happiness and all ends with praise of God's mercy for the pure of heart.

The opera is set in a Bohemian forest and calls for a virtuoso performance from the special effects department – with thunder, lightning, shattering glass, strange animals and birds, demonic manifestations. The music foreshadows Wagner with its leitmotifs. Particular use is made of the wind instruments – the horns capture the atmosphere of the German forest, trombones accompany the Hermit, the clarinet characterises Agatha and the low register of the flute is the demon Samiel.

The overture sets the scene for the opera and there are marvellous folksong-like melodies and dance tunes throughout for chorus and soloists. The most famous single aria is Agatha's prayer 'Leise, leise' ('Softly, softly'). Berlioz (not an easy man to please) used all the superlatives in the book to describe the opera:

> From the beginning of the overture to the last chord of the final chorus," he said, "it is impossible for me to find a bar the omission of which or the change of which I would find desirable. Intelligence, imagination, genius shine everywhere...

Overtures

In addition to *Der Freischütz*, there are other Weber overtures which should not be missed. The opera *Oberon* contains some of Weber's most delightful music and we are given a good sampling of it in the overture, which is a very popular concert piece. It opens with a horn call which becomes associated with Oberon throughout the work (that leitmotif again!). The overture to *Euryanthe* is also well worthy of your attention, and a personal favourite of mine is the charming little overture to *Abu Hassan*, not so much an opera as a Singspiel - a German expression for a stage work with spoken dialogue and folk-like tunes.

Clarinet Concerto No. 1 in F Minor

Weber made a huge contribution to the development of opera in Germany, but he also wrote some great music for clarinet. This came about because there was a brilliant clarinettist called Heinrich Bärmann in the court orchestra in Munich and the King of Bavaria, no less, commissioned Weber to write concertos for him. There are two concertos and one concertino (little concerto), the pick of them being 'Concerto No. 1', which is one of the pearls in the wind repertoire. The slow sections are lyrical and romantic – guaranteed to melt the stormiest heart – and the rondo finale is one of the most tuneful, infectious movements you'll ever hear.

Invitation to the Dance

The orchestral piece which we now know as 'Invitation to the Dance' started life in 1819 as a piano piece by Weber. It was orchestrated 22 years later by Berlioz, when some ballet music was needed for a production of *Der Freischütz* at the Paris Opéra (Weber couldn't do it himself because he had died fifteen years earlier). The central section of 'Invitation to the Dance' was also used by the choreographer Fokine for his ballet *La Spectre de la Rose*. The slow introduction is the gentleman's invitation to the lady, then comes the dance proper followed by his courteous thanks and farewell.

GIOACHINO ROSSINI
(1792-1868)

Rossini must have got some of his music from his parents. His father was a trumpeter and his mother a singer, though neither of them was exceptionally gifted. Rossini Senior was in fact town trumpeter of Pesaro, a sort of musical town crier. He also had the more mundane job of inspector of slaughterhouses. When his wife didn't have a singing job she worked as a seamstress in people's homes.

Even before the young Gioachino entered the Bologna Conservatory in 1806, he had learned to play the piano and cello, performed as a singer and composed chamber works, overtures and sacred music. He soon began to make a name for himself in Bologna. Commissions for operas came in and by the end of his 21st year he had already written ten operas for various Italian theatres. These were mostly one-acts, but his first full-scale opera, *Tancredi*, went down well in Venice. Then came *The Italian Girl in Algiers* which made him a superstar. All the major opera houses wanted operas from him – Naples, Rome, Milan – and later came commissions from Vienna, Paris and London. Rossini travelled with his wife (the Spanish soprano Isabella Colbran) from one city to the other and was cheered and fêted wherever he went.

Then, in 1829, at the age of 37, Rossini settled in Paris. He put six months of concentrated labour into the opera *William Tell*, which resulted in severe insomnia, nervousness and eye-strain. He obviously decided that he didn't want to go through the same sort of thing again, because he never attempted to write another opera. He lived another 39 years but composed only one substantial work – the *Stabat Mater*. He lived the good life, enjoying good food, wine and conversation and sometimes entertaining his guests with little trifles which he composed for the piano (a number of these later found their way into the tuneful ballet *La Boutique Fantasque*).

Many theories have been put forward as to why Rossini threw in the towel at the age of 37, but the truth probably lay in what he himself is supposed to have said:

I wrote operas when melodies overwhelmed me, when they came searching for me. But one day I noticed that they did

*not come any more, that I had to search for them. And that
is the moment when I gave it up.*

Rossini and his wife Isabella had parted company in 1830. She
was seven years his senior and had sung the leading rôles in
many of his operas. Since she brought him a substantial dowry
cynics had looked on the marriage as just another of Rossini's
cunning business deals. After the split-up, Rossini didn't want
for female company. A lady called Olympe was happy to minister to all his creature comforts and he eventually married her in
1846. I'm sure he left her well provided for after his death in
1868, but he did leave quite a proportion of his fortune to musical endowments and foundations. He was particularly keen to
encourage composers with a turn for melody. There was a brilliant turnout at his funeral, as befitting a man with so many
honours and decorations and there are portraits and busts of
him today in many of Europe's leading musical institutions.

Rossini – A Middlebrow Mix

The Barber of Seville

First nights in the theatre can be nervewracking affairs, but few can have been as disastrous as the first night of *The Barber*. A number of other composers had based operas on the play by Beaumarchais and one of them was in Rome in 1816. His name was Giovanni Paisiello and he said very rude things about Rossini. In fact, he did more than that – he organised his cronies to sabotage the performance. There was constant hooting and jeering – so much noise that the singers could hardly hear the orchestra. Then little things began to go wrong. Almaviva tried to tune his guitar for the serenade to Rosina and a string snapped in his face. Don Basilio tripped on his first entrance and had to sing from a prone position. Another singer fell through a trapdoor. To crown it all, a cat wandered onto the stage during the first act finale. (I know how that feels - I was in the middle of a solo piece in the Gaiety Theatre when Robbie, the theatre cat, sat down behind me and began her ablutions. It was a funny piece, but I couldn't understand the audience's uncontrolled hilarity on that particular night.) Anyway, the première was a disaster and Rossini went home in despair. Happily, everything went well on the second night. The composer was cheered and congratulated and within a few years the opera had become one of the most popular in the world.

The opera is set in 17th-century Seville. Count Almaviva (tenor) has fallen for Rosina (soprano), the rich young ward of Dr Bartolo (bass), who wants to marry her himself. The Count does not want to reveal his true identity, so he pretends to be Lindoro, a poor student and Rosina is very taken with the handsome youth. At the suggestion of the resourceful barber Figaro (baritone), the Count gains entrance into Bartolo's home by disguising himself as a drunken soldier looking for lodgings and then as a music teacher substituting for Rosina's regular teacher Don Basilio (bass), who is a friend and supporter of Bartolo. In the end the Count admits his true identity to a delighted Rosina and a notary who has been summoned by old Bartolo to marry him to Rosina is forced by Figaro to marry her instead to the Count. With no choice remaining to him, Bartolo blesses the marriage and is consoled by being allowed to keep Rosina's dowry.

Among the outstanding numbers is 'Largo al factotum' –
Figaro's brilliant account of how he loves being a jack of all trades.
'Uno voce poco fa' is one of the great coloratura showpieces in
which Rosina writes a letter saying how she has been attracted to
the voice of Lindoro. 'Pace e gioia' is the Count's aria in the guise
of Don Alonso, a student of the singing master and 'Contro un
cor' is the duet in which the young lovers express their mutual
affection. The overture, of course, is a must.

At one stage during his retirement, Rossini set down a
number of recipes for the writing of overtures. The first and
invariable rule, he said, was to wait for the eve of the first
performance before composing one. Nothing is better for
inspiration than necessity. In the case of *The Barber of Seville*,
though, the overture was not composed on the eve of the first
performance but a good while before that. It had in fact been
used in two of Rossini's earlier operas, neither of which was
likely to be heard very often. So why not take some of the good
tunes and recycle them? After all, as Rossini knew so well, good
tunes can be enjoyed over and over again.

We're told that Rossini composed *The Barber of Seville* in thirteen days. Asked if such a feat were possible, the composer
Donizetti is said to have replied, "Why not? Rossini is so lazy."
Donizetti himself tossed off operas – 75 of them – with indecent
speed and nonchalance.

La Cenerentola ('Cinderella')

This opera is the runner-up in popularity to *The Barber of Seville*
and I don't need to outline the plot – everyone knows the story
of poor Cinders and her ugly stepsisters. It deserves special
mention because Cinderella is one of the great roles for mezzo-
soprano, and if you would like me to recommend one I would
unhesitatingly go for the great Spaniard Teresa Berganza. If you
are a regular middlebrow you will know that Señora Berganza
sends shivers down my spine (she is to me what Meryl Streep is
to Gay Byrne). Of more recent vintage there is the Italian Cecilia
Bartoli, who has attained great popularity and is one of the
current stars of the New York Metropolitan Opera

Overtures

The Thieving Magpie

Many of Rossini's overtures are in the concert repertoire, even though the operas to which they were attached are never heard. Rossini believed in getting value out of a good overture and, when he could, he simply dusted off an old one and added the title of the new opera. Most impresarios were wise to him, though, and demanded their money's worth. With 'The Thieving Magpie', Rossini cut things a bit fine. He came down to the opera house on the day of the première, smiling and cheerful, saying to the manager what a nice idea it would be to have an opera without an overture for a change, especially since he hadn't written it yet. Unfortunately the manager didn't think it was a good idea at all; in fact, he thought it was the worst idea he'd heard in years. What's more, he locked Rossini up in the attic of the opera house with pen, paper and four trusty stage hands. The pen and paper were for Rossini to write the overture and the four trusty stage hands were for throwing him out the window in case he didn't. But he did, and as fast as he could dash off the pages, Rossini flung them out the window. Below them in the courtyard, a small army of copyists scooped them up and wrote out the parts for the orchestra while the impatient impresario danced around tearing his hair out. Rossini boasted that all his impresarios were bald by the age of 30.

'The Thieving Magpie' was the very first overture I heard at a symphony concert, the one I told you about in the Introduction. That was the moment when I became a middlebrow, though I hadn't yet invented the word. This overture exemplifies as well, if not better, than any other the crescendo for which Rossini was famous and which led to his nickname Signor Crescendo. The opera was first produced in 1817 at La Scala and it earned Rossini, who was already acclaimed in Venice, his first ovation from a Milanese audience. The magpie of the title causes all sorts of trouble by stealing a silver spoon belonging to a Florentine lady, who promptly has a servant-girl condemned to the scaffold for the offence. The rolling of the executioner's ceremonial drum opens the overture, but thereafter all is light and gay and I need hardly add that the innocent girl does not lose her head after all.

William Tell

One of the first grand operas was Rossini's 1829 extravaganza 'William Tell', which relied for much of its effect on crowd scenes and pageantry. This overture has been called a little symphony, and it certainly contains enough variety of mood, melody and colour to justify the description. It has four distinct movements as well: a romantic section first, a lovely cello solo, then the Alpine storm, followed by a pastoral sequence with beautiful passages for cor anglais and flute. The overture comes to its stirring conclusion with the celebrated finale depicting a fierce onslaught by Swiss soldiery. Someone has said that the definition of a highbrow is someone who can listen to the 'William Tell' overture without thinking of the Lone Ranger. That places me firmly in the middlebrow camp – again.

Other recommended Rossini overtures are *Il Signor Bruschino*, not beloved of string players, who are asked to tap their bows on the music stands, *The Silken Ladder* (an absolute gem), *The Italian Girl in Algiers*, *Semiramide* – I could go on but I suggest you just get a CD of Rossini overtures and listen to them all.

Piano Pieces

When he gave up writing operas, Rossini enjoyed the good life, but as we've noted, liked to play little pieces for his guests. Some of these pieces were brilliantly orchestrated by the Italian Ottorino Respighi for the ballet *La Boutique Fantasque* ('The Fantastic Toy Shop') which was first performed by the Diaghilev company in London in 1919. Most of the dances are performed by various dolls who inhabit a toyshop in Nice. Having suffered various vicissitudes, all turns out well in the end as the dolls and their maker get rid of the undesirable customers and celebrate their triumph. Best known pieces are probably the 'Clog Dance', the 'Tarantella' and the 'Can-Can'. Very different but also delightful are the orchestrations of Rossini's piano pieces by Benjamin Britten in the two suites 'Matinées Musicales' and 'Soirées Musicales'.

GAETANO DONIZETTI
(1797-1848)

Donizetti earns his place in the Top 40 through giving us at least three wonderful operas. He had a great gift for melody, and was certainly the speediest composer of operas, turning them out at a rate of knots. Mendelssohn, a slightly younger contemporary, said of him:

> *Donizetti finishes an opera in ten days. It may be hissed, to be sure, but that doesn't matter as it is paid for all the same and then he can go about having a good time.*

Donizetti entered the army to escape practising law, but his aim was always to be a composer. He had had a musical training and while in barracks he wrote an opera which marked him out as a person of great talent. He was given a contract by a Neapolitan impresario and started composing operas in earnest. His first big success was *Anna Bolena* in Milan in 1830, which won him commissions from all the leading Italian opera houses. He composed 65 operas in all, at one time turning out four or five a year. He had an incredible facility which resembled Rossini's in that it was prolific and produced easily singable tunes. He had picked Rossini as a model, a shrewd thing to do, but he never attained his compatriot's stature in the musical world.

Donizetti carried on a running battle against censors who had an embargo on religious topics on stage and wouldn't countenance any suggestions that Catholic kings and queens might be subject to human frailties. His operas on English subjects passed muster as they usually dealt with the Protestant Tudors. By nature, however, he was an affable man who got on well with people, but an awful lot of misfortune came his way. None of his three children lived more than a few days and his beloved wife Virginia died in 1839 at the age of 29 during a dreadful outbreak of cholera. His own health began to deteriorate in 1843. He suffered violent headaches, depression and hallucinations and spent eighteen months in a lunatic asylum. According to a report he would sit motionless in full dress clothes, his hat in his hand, a tragic picture of insanity. He was released into the custody of his brother in Bergamo but didn't last much longer, dying in 1848 at the age of 51.

Donizetti – A Middlebrow Mix

Lucia di Lammermoor

Based on Walter Scott's novel *The Bride of Lammermoor*, the story takes place in Scotland about 1700. Lucia is in love with Edgar of Ravenswood, who is an enemy of her brother Lord Henry Ashton. Henry wants Lucia to marry Sir Arthur Bucklow for political reasons and forges a letter to make Lucia believe that Edgar has been unfaithful. Lucia consents to the marriage and has just signed the wedding contract when Edgar returns unexpectedly from France. He curses Lucia for her treachery with the result that she goes mad and during the wedding festivities she murders her new husband and expires in front of the guests with the bloodstained dagger in her hand. Edgar has already decided that he no longer wants to live without Lucia but, learning of her death, he proceeds without delay to stab himself.

 Lucia is filled with memorable melodies but the two most celebrated sections are the mad scene, which can be a tour de force for the soprano if she can act as well as sing. I wish I had seen Maria Callas in the rôle – she had everything. The other must is the sextet, which is one of the most wondrous pieces of ensemble writing in all opera and deservedly high on the hit list. It comes at the end of Act II, when the guests are assembled for the wedding of Lucia and Arthur and Edgar turns up. They express their conflicting emotions while the other principals add their comments and the voices blend miraculously.

Don Pasquale

This is Donizetti's comic masterpiece. Ernesto wants to marry the young widow Norina, but his uncle Don Pasquale disapproves and throws him out of the house. The Don wants to get married himself in order to sire some more direct heirs. Dr Malatesta produces a bride for him, claiming that she is his own sister. She is in fact Norina, who leads Pasquale a merry dance and torments him to such an extent that he is delighted to get rid of her and agree to her marriage to his nephew.

There are wonderful moments in the opera. First of all, be sure to listen to the overture, a sparkling piece that quotes a number of tunes heard later.

Highlights include 'Bella siccome un angelo' in Act I, when Malatesta tells Don Pasquale of the perfect girl for him, one who is indeed 'perfect as an angel'; 'Com'é gentil' in Act III, Ernesto's serenade to his beloved Norina and 'Tornami a dir', the lovers' beautiful duet, also in Act III.

L'Elisir d'Amore ('The Elixir of Love')

The gentle and penniless Nemorino is hopelessly in love with Adina, who shows far more interest in Sergeant Belcore. Nemorino takes a love potion, being assured by the quack Dr Dulcamara that it will make him irresistible. All it does is make him tipsy, but when the village girls hear that Nemorino has inherited a fortune they fawn over him. Seeing this, Adina decides that he must have something after all, so she decides that she is in love with him. The most surprised person in sight is Dr Dulcamara.

Again, there are lovely melodies in this opera, but the aria we all know and love is 'Una furtiva lagrima' ('A furtive tear'), in Act II. Nemorino piles on the grief in this tenor love song, aided by a most affecting bassoon obbligato.

Other Donizetti arias to note include 'Spirto gentil', the tenor aria from *La Favorita* and 'O Luce di qu'est anima', a terrific coloratura piece for soprano from *Linda di Chamonix*.

VINCENZO BELLINI
(1801-1835)

With the exception of Schubert, Vincenzo Bellini was the shortest-lived of our Top 40 composers. He is remembered for three operas which have provided starring roles for prima donnas – notably, in the last half-century, Maria Callas and Joan Sutherland. These two divas contributed greatly to a revival of interest in Bellini after a long period of near-eclipse. It is not hard to see why they so loved his works. He wrote spectacular arias calling for great vocal agility, but he also made sure that each display piece fitted its setting and came at some climactic emotional moment. This had not always been the case with his popular contemporary and rival Donizetti or, indeed, the great Rossini.

Bellini was born in Sicily where his father and grandfather were both professional musicians. He then studied in Naples where he had his first taste of success with his operas before moving on to Milan and Venice. He was inclined to be unreasonably jealous when an opera by a rival was acclaimed, but at least Rossini was not a threat, as he decided to rest on his laurels just when Bellini was really coming into his own. Rossini was in fact a great help to his younger countryman. He recommended that Bellini compose an opera specifically for the Théâtre Italien in Paris, with which he himself had long been associated. The resulting opera, *I Puritani*, was rapturously received there on its première in 1835.

Bellini had arrived in Paris a couple of years before, having left Italy to escape the embarrassment of a love affair with a lady whose husband had found them out. He had already had great success with *La Sonnambula* and *Norma*, both in Italy and as far afield as Russia and America. The stars of that time (the 1830s) also recognised these operas as great vehicles for dazzling their audiences. Bellini was not to know that he would never return to Italy. The success of *I Puritani* gave him a position in Parisian musical life which he himself described as "second only to Rossini" (though no longer composing, Rossini remained the presiding genius of Parisian opera).

Who knows what heights Bellini might have reached had his great talent not been snuffed out at such an early age? Compared to Mozart or Schubert, his output was minuscule. He had only begun to realise his potential when he contracted acute gas-troenteritis. This was complicated by an abscess of the liver and resulted in his death at the age of 34.

Bellini – A Middlebrow Mix

La Sonnambula ('The Sleepwalker')

Bellini was almost exclusively a composer of operas – he wrote eleven. Three of these are outstanding and perhaps the most popular is *La Sonnambula*. First produced in Milan in 1831, this made the composer's reputation throughout Europe. The principal rôle was written for Giuditta Pasta, one of the superstar sopranos of the era. Bellini also wrote the title rôle of *Norma* for her and referred many times to her "encyclopaedic artistry".

The opera is set in a Swiss village. The orphan Amina is to marry the wealthy farmer Alvino. However, her propensity for sleepwalking gets her into hot water. She is discovered in the bedroom of Count Rodolfo; Elvino calls off the wedding and makes plans to marry another. Rodolfo tries to explain the phenomenon of somnambulism and the innocence of Amina's nocturnal visit but nobody is convinced until Amina is spotted walking perilously on rooftops. She is obviously asleep, so all is forgiven and order is restored.

This may sound like the stuff of farce and might indeed have been treated as such had the composer been Donizetti. However, Bellini manages to make it charming and highly romantic. The central rôle is a great challenge as the singer/actress has to be convincing while asleep. This was no bother to Maria Callas – the definitive interpreter of the three great Bellini rôles (though Joan Sutherland has her devotees). I have seen neither of these remarkable ladies, so only know them through recordings. The Sutherland voice is sweeter but Callas wins hands down in the acting department. The highlight of *La Sonnambula* is the sleepwalking scene in Act II, the climax of the action.

Norma

Norma was also premièred in Milan in 1831, with Pasta in the leading role. It was not an instant success, the composer blamed this on hostile factions in the audience. However, it soon conquered Europe and is considered Bellini's greatest achievement.

The action takes place in Gaul during the pre-Christian Roman occupation. Norma is a druid priestess who has an unhappy love affair with the Roman pro-consul Pollione and bears his children. He switches his affections to Adalgisa, a novice priestess, who declares her loyalty to Norma. The priority for the Gauls is to destroy the Romans, but the deity requires a sacrifice. Norma decides that she herself will be the victim. Entrusting her children to the care of her father, the chief druid, she mounts a blazing funeral pyre and is joined in the flames by a remorseful Pollione.

The most celebrated number in *Norma* is 'Casta diva' ('Chaste goddess'). It seems that Giuditta Pasta at first disliked this great hymn to the moon but was won over. It's a slow, beautiful melody in which the troubled heroine expresses her longing for peace and purity and while moving us the diva can also dazzle us with her virtuosity.

I Puritani ('The Puritans')

The story was loosely based on a novel by Sir Walter Scott, set during England's Civil War period. Elvira, daughter of a Puritan governor-general, is to marry Lord Arthur, a Royalist. Her father disapproves but is unwilling to force his wishes on her. Arthur disappears just before the wedding (duty calls, he has to rescue the Queen) and poor Elvira is distraught. In fact, she loses her cool to such an extent that yet another opportunity arises for an operatic 'mad scene'. News comes that Parliament has condemned Arthur to the scaffold, which doesn't help matters. However, he returns to his beloved and is saved from execution when the Civil War ends in the nick of time. The Stuarts have been defeated, a general pardon is issued and Elvira miraculously recovers her sanity.

My favourite two pieces from the opera are the arias 'A te o cara' and 'Son vergin vezzosa'. The first is a wonderful tenor aria from Act I in which Arthur expresses his great happiness before his wedding and compares it with the time he had to woo Elvira in secret due to political differences. The second is a sparkling coloratura piece in which Elvira sings of her happiness – here Sutherland definitely gets the vote over Callas.

HECTOR BERLIOZ
(1803-1869)

Berlioz was a larger-than-life character, but personally and musically some of this contemporaries held him in exaggerated contempt, one so-called authority declaring that, "What M. Berlioz does has nothing to do with art." He was, of course, a rebel. He felt that he had to break away from the accepted musical forms and express himself with new patterns, new sounds. He showed an audacity which was resented by a few composers of the time – notably Liszt and Wagner.

Berlioz's father was a country doctor and he wanted young Hector to follow in his footsteps, but this wasn't to be. He did actually start medical studies in Paris but the dissection of corpses disgusted him. He entered the Paris Conservatoire, to the horror of his father who left him to his own financial devices. Berlioz managed to keep himself going by taking on a variety of musical chores.

Even at that early stage, Berlioz was a rebel. He refused to conform to any of the rules laid down by his professors. There is a story of the director of the Conservatoire, Cherubini, chasing him around the library tables in the course of a heated argument. Cherubini was not a man to be crossed, and he used his considerable influence to prevent Berlioz from achieving an early success. Berlioz was in fact 27 when he was finally awarded the prestigious Prix de Rome, which enabled him to live and work in Italy for a while. However, he did not stay for the full three-year period, as he was homesick and decided to return to Paris.

Berlioz was never able to earn a living from his compositions. His main income came from music journalism – he became recognised as perhaps the greatest musical critic of his time. He wrote a lot about his own works too, in an attempt to have them understood and appreciated. In his later life he made money from conducting his works, insisting on having the most enormous orchestral forces at his disposal. His ideal was 500 instruments.

Berlioz composed nothing in the last seven years of his life. This was an unhappy period for him. His marriage to Harriet Smithson (an Irish actress with whom he was infatuated and who inspired much of his music) had broken up after a brief, stormy passage. His second wife was an Italian opera singer (everything about the stage fascinated him!) but she died suddenly in 1862. He also lost his son Louis at sea, and his last opera, *Les Troyens*, was booed off the stage in Paris. He died a lonely and disappointed man – to quote from his memoirs:

> *I have neither hopes nor illusions nor great thoughts left. I am alone, and every hour I say to Death, "When you will".*

Death obliged in 1869 and put this volatile innovator out of his misery.

Berlioz – A Middlebrow Mix

Symphonie Fantastique

With his 'Symphonie Fantastique', Berlioz established a new ideal of descriptive orchestral music. The work was first performed at the Paris Conservatoire in 1830 to a very mixed reception indeed. Some hailed it as the "new music", while others openly despised it.

The piece arose out of Berlioz's overwhelming passion for Harriet Smithson, an Irish actress from County Clare who appeared in Paris for a season of Shakespeare plays. Berlioz had seen her as Ophelia and Juliet and fallen madly in love with her. He wrote her letters, which she ignored, thus denying him the opportunity to demonstrate his ardent feelings for her. A rumour that she was engaged to be married made Berlioz so violently jealous that he felt compelled to express his unrequited love in a symphony. The work is subtitled 'An episode in the life of an artist', and Berlioz himself wrote explicit notes on the ideas he wanted to express. He asked the listener to imagine the over-sensitive young musician poisoning himself with opium and falling into a dream full of extraordinary visions. The beloved woman herself becomes for him a melody, a so-called *idée fixe*, which he hears everywhere.

There are five movements, or scenes.

1.   Dreams, Passions: 'He has moments of anxiety, of jealous fury.'
2.   The Ball: 'He sees his beloved during a brilliant ball.' (This piece is an irresistible waltz.)
3.   Scenes in the Country: 'The playing of two shepherds one summer evening renders him calm – but she appears again!'
4.   March to the Scaffold: 'He dreams that he has killed his beloved and is being marched to the guillotine.'
5.   The Witches' Sabbath: 'He sees himself surrounded by a host of fearsome, grotesque spectres and she is one of them!' (The use of the 'Dies Irae' is memorable here.)

As an afternote, Berlioz remained obsessed with Harriet for another few years, but finally cured himself by marrying her in 1833.

Roman Carnival Overture

This marvellous overture was originally written as a prelude to the second act of the opera *Benvenuto Cellini*. There is a lovely melody associated with the lovers, and an exhilarating sound-picture of Carnival festivities – a middlebrow must.

The Damnation of Faust

This is a mighty 'dramatic legend' for solo voices, chorus and orchestra, with three orchestral pieces which are middlebrow favourites. The 'Hungarian (or 'Rakoczy') March' originally had nothing to do with Faust. It was written as a tribute to the Hungarian Count Rakoczy and based on a popular revolutionary song. It was so effective that Berlioz invented a scene in *The Damnation of Faust* to accommodate it. The 'Dance of the Sylphs' is a dainty waltz which pictures several sylphs executing a dance near Faust, who has fallen asleep on the bank of a river. 'Minuet of the Will-o'-the-Wisps' describes how, at the command of Mephistopheles, a group of spirits performs a picturesque dance under Marguerite's window, accompanied by fluttering woodwinds

'Villanelle'

This is the prettiest and most popular of the six songs in the Romantic cycle 'Les nuits d'été ('Summer nights') for solo voice and orchestra. Our own Bernadette Greevy can not be excluded in this one.

FELIX MENDELSSOHN
(1809-1847)

Almost alone among the great composers, Felix Mendelssohn never wanted for anything as a boy. He was the son of Abraham Mendelssohn, a rich Jewish banker, who provided the best musical tutors money could buy for Felix and his equally talented sister Fanny. There was even a private orchestra to conduct in the back garden of the house in Berlin on Sunday afternoons! By the age of fifteen, Mendelssohn had already composed symphonies, chamber works and an opera. At seventeen he composed the great octet and the overture to *A Midsummer Night's Dream* and with these he was well on his way to becoming one of the most admired composers in Europe.

Mendelssohn was outstandingly gifted in more ways than one. He was a brilliant linguist, he wrote poetry and sketched and was also something of a philosopher. However, music took precedence. He had an incredible amount of natural ability and in addition to being a world-class composer he was also a virtuoso pianist, a superb organist and an accomplished string player.

Mendelssohn's graduation present from his proud parents was a three-year Grand Tour of Europe. He was a handsome, charming young man and he made friends wherever he went. He was particularly loved in London, where he became a favourite of the Royal Family. He also gathered impressions which were later translated into works like 'The Hebrides' (or 'In Fingal's Cave') overture and the 'Scottish' and 'Italian' symphonies.

At the age of 26 Mendelssohn was appointed conductor of the famous Gewandhaus Orchestra in Leipzig. He was very happy here, both in his home life with his wife and five children and with the musical giants who flocked to his side. It is said that he reigned over the orchestra with a charming autocracy. Rossini and Chopin visited him, Schumann was his close friend. Ferdinand David, for whom he wrote the sublime 'Violin Concerto', was his orchestra leader. He founded the Leipzig Conservatory to which he attracted a brilliant staff of teachers, and also travelled regularly to Berlin and Dresden to conduct – as well as continuing to visit Britain.

Mendelssohn had to get up very early in the morning to give

himself time to compose. He did, of course, conduct some of his
own works in Leipzig, but mostly it was Bach, Mozart, Haydn,
Handel and Beethoven whose music was heard there, and he
brought the music of these great composers from obscurity to
public fame. Mendelssohn also presented the first performance
of Schubert's 'Symphony in C', the 'Great C Major' and was almost single-handedly responsible for reviving an interest in the
music of Bach with a performance of the *St Matthew Passion* – a
work he had first mounted at the age of 20.

The composer was a workaholic and his hectic schedule took
its toll. He was only 38 when he suffered a series of small strokes,
and was mourned worldwide when he died in 1847.

The music of Mendelssohn has had its detractors – one being
George Bernard Shaw, when he was music critic for the *London
Star* under the pseudonym of Corno di Bassetto. Well, perhaps
Mendelssohn lacks sufficient depth for highbrows, but the public
has always been on his side. His music is easy on the ear and
has a charm and delicacy second to none. The violinist Jascha
Heifetz said:

> *If it is conceivable that the music of Mendelssohn can die,
> then all music can die.*

Mendelssohn – A Middlebrow Mix

Symphony No. 4 (the 'Italian')

In 1830 Mendelssohn set off on a tour of Italy, which lasted over
a year. He had intended to spend his mornings composing and
practising, but the distractions were many and varied and he
found it difficult to adhere to his schedule. However, within a
year he did write to his sister:

> *I have once more begun to compose with great vigour and the
> Italian symphony makes rapid progress. It will be the most
> amusing piece I have yet composed.*

However, after the initial inspiration, the symphony didn't come
easily to Mendelssohn. It took him two years to complete the
work and during that time he complained that it was costing
him "the bitterest moments I have ever endured or could have

imagined". The symphony sounds so spontaneous and effervescent, full of lovely melodies from beginning to end, that it is hard for us today to imagine those difficulties.

The first movement has us smiling from the word go and is joyous throughout; the finale is in the style of a *saltarello*, an ancient Italian dance whose name derives from the word *saltare*, meaning 'to skip' or 'to jump'.

Violin Concerto No. 2 in E Minor

It was the celebrated violinist Ferdinand David who urged Mendelssohn to write a violin concerto. "I have the liveliest desire to write one for you," Mendelssohn replied, "and if I have a few propitious days I shall bring you something of the sort." Those few days stretched into five years, but when the concerto did appear in 1845, with David as soloist, it was greeted with great acclaim and has probably become the most popular of all.

David made many suggestions to Mendelssohn and the composer was very happy to receive them and to take the expert's advice. Mendelssohn actually stated his wish that the work should be easy for a skilled violinist to play. That makes a nice change, I think. Some composers seem to have been intent on making their compositions as difficult as possible for the soloist.

The concerto may not be exactly easy, but it is certainly 'violinistic'. That's a term I've heard professional violinists use to describe a work which lies comfortably within the manual range. It doesn't exclude virtuosity by any means, but it does exclude the awkward stretches and leaps which are sometimes demanded by composers who don't understand the instrument. The concerto has been described as "bearing the charm of eternal youth" and has a number of innovations. Never before in a violin concerto had the soloist made his first entry before the orchestra had outlined the themes, but here the orchestra has barely announced its presence before the soloist soars right in with the first melody. There is no actual break between movements either. At the end of the first movement the bassoonist holds one note of the final chord and before we know it we are into the andante, a radiant "song without words", one of the most sublime and familiar pieces ever penned for the violin. Then again, there's a transitional passage leading into the vivacious finale which recaptures the high spirits of *A Midsummer Night's Dream*.

In Fingal's Cave (or The Hebrides) Overture

Mendelssohn was only twenty when he visited Scotland in 1829. He was bowled over by the Hebrides, and on the bleak island of Staffa he made notes for a composition. Over a year later these were fleshed out and became the great overture that is known as 'The Hebrides', or 'In Fingal's Cave'. It is a wonderful musical seascape: just close your eyes and picture the savage beauty of this remote place, the sound of seagulls and the salt spray cascading over the cliffs. It begins with gentle ripples, builds up to a spectacular storm, and then subsides again with tranquillity. It's surely one of the most evocative pieces ever to be heard on *Music for Middlebrows*.

A Midsummer Night's Dream (overture and incidental music)

When Mendelssohn was seventeen he read Shakespeare's play *A Midsummer Night's Dream* and was fascinated by its fairytale world. His fascination found expression in an overture which was first performed in the garden of the Mendelssohn house in Berlin. The composer confided later that he improvised it "on the piano of a neighbour – a beautiful lady who lived nearby". It's a remarkable overture for one so young, yet when asked years later to describe what he had attempted to depict, Mendelssohn could only say that the music followed the play rather closely in mood and imagery. Most fairytale music is light and happy – but this overture is far more than fun music. It has a heroic nature and a brilliance which set a standard for atmospheric music. Those in the know say that no-one before or after – not even Mozart – produced a work of such magnificence at so early an age.

It was sixteen years before Mendelssohn returned to *A Midsummer Night's Dream*. King Friedrich Wilhelm IV of Prussia commissioned him to compose incidental music for a production of the play at a new theatre in Potsdam. Amazingly, the 33-year-old was able to re-kindle the youthful flame of genius and the thirteen additional pieces seem perfectly matched in tone and style to the original.

Of the later pieces, four are usually grouped with the overture to form a suite: the scherzo, nocturne, intermezzo and wedding march. The scherzo is one of the most enchanting pieces of music ever written – a sound picture world of scurrying elves and goblins, with the flute playing a major rôle. The intermezzo is in a minor key and evokes the darker side of the forest, while the nocturne is pensive love music with the main melody given to the horns and bassoons. Then comes the beloved march that has escorted more people to the altar than any comparable piece of music (the march from Wagner's *Lohengrin* comes a close second). The wedding march celebrates the triple marriage which forms the happy dénouement of Shakespeare's play.

Piano Works

The 'Concerto No. 1 in G' is marvellous – particularly the finale. Also with orchestra is the Capriccio Brillant, which more than lives up to its title. For solo piano the 'Songs Without Words' are a must. There are 48 altogether, the most popular being 'Spring Song' (Opus 62, No. 6) and 'The Bee's Wedding' (Opus 67, No. 4). Another great piece for solo piano is 'Andante and Rondo Capriccioso'.

Octet in E Flat for Strings

Of all the chamber music, this octet is outstanding. Mendelssohn composed it when he was sixteen, before even the overture to *A Midsummer Night's Dream* and it heralded his greatness. It's a long work with four spacious movements, taking about 40 minutes to play. As an introduction or hors d'oeuvre, listen to the scherzo, which is utterly irresistible, at least on a par with the better known *Midsummer* scherzo.

Elijah

For those who like big oratorios, this is one to be savoured. It is not quite as popular as it once was, but still makes a big impact in the concert hall – particularly with its monumental choruses.

FRÉDÉRIC CHOPIN
(1810-1849)

Chopin was born in Poland of a Polish mother who was the daughter of an impoverished nobleman. His father was a Frenchman who taught French to the well-to-do. When Chopin first played the piano in public at the age of eight, he was hailed in Warsaw as the 'new Mozart' — a bit over the top, perhaps, but then one would think it was enough to be the first Chopin.

At the age of twenty Chopin left Poland. Elsner, his former teacher at the Warsaw Conservatory, presented him with a silver goblet filled with Polish soil, as though foreseeing that his pupil would never see his native land again. Chopin cherished this farewell gift throughout his life, and it was buried with him — well, the soil was anyway, whatever about the goblet.

Chopin's first port of call was Vienna, where he was very unhappy. It was here that he heard that Warsaw had fallen to the Russians and penned the passionate 'Revolutionary Etude' (Opus 10, No. 12). Little more than 100 years later, in 1939, it was the last piece of music defiantly broadcast on Warsaw Radio before the Germans over-ran the city. Chopin then visited a number of German cities, considered visiting the United States but ended up in Paris where he soon found himself at home. Paris in the 1830s boasted more artists than Aosdana. Painters, poets, playwrights – all sorts of intellectuals were there. Names that come to mind include Victor Hugo, Honoré Balzac, Lamartine, Heinrich Heine and the painter Ferdinand Delacroix. There were musicians too – Berlioz, Liszt, Rossini and Mendelsshon from time-to-time.

Another person who was there was Georges Sand – famous novelist, cigar-smoker, wearer of men's clothes. She had had affairs with a number of literary greats but she and Chopin became an item for about ten years. Chopin had felt heart-flutterings for gentle maidens like Maria Wodzinska, but Madame Sand was a different kettle of fish altogether. She was the dominant personality, a political activist opposed to tradition and convention, while Chopin was a sensitive soul not unduly concerned with social justice.

The most famous episode of their relationship was the winter they spent in Majorca. This was supposed to be for the good of Chopin's health, but it nearly killed him – it was wet and miserable the whole time and they were living in primitive conditions in a deserted monastery. The only good things to come out of the whole gloomy episode were some preludes — the most famous, ironically, being the 'Raindrop', (Opus 28, No. 4), the constantly repeated A-flat suggesting the dripping of raindrops.

The relationship with Georges Sand ended in 1847 and it still remains something of a mystery. Some writers have wondered if there was a physical aspect to it at all — perhaps it was just an intriguing intellectual romance. Did she inspire him and encourage him to write all that marvellous music? Anyway he went quickly downhill after she left his life. He went to London where the fog aggravated the weakness of his lungs. He crept back to Paris where he died of tuberculosis in 1849 – yet another of those great composers who never celebrated a 50th birthday.

Chopin was one of the finest pianists of all time, but it seems that his legendary reputation was built up on the strength of a

mere 30 or 30 public appearances. He once confided to Franz
Liszt,

> *I am not suited for concert-giving, the public intimidate me.*
> *You have the force to overwhelm them.*

In fact, as soon as he was firmly established as a composer in
Paris, he was happy to retire from the concert platform and leave
that field to the more extrovert Liszt and Thalberg.

Chopin is rightly known as the "poet of the piano" – he
became the outstanding exponent of lyrical romanticism in
music. Artur Rubinstein (one of the great Chopin interpreters)
has written:

> *When the first notes of Chopin sound through the concert*
> *hall, there is a happy sigh of recognition. All over the world*
> *men and women know his music – they love it, they are moved*
> *by it. When I play Chopin I know I speak directly to the hearts*
> *of the people.*

Every one of Chopin's works was written either for solo piano or
a combination that includes the piano. There are two concertos,
but neither of these is considered extra-special – writing for the
orchestra was not his thing. There are three sonatas – the second,
in B flat minor, having the famous funeral march which is known
to millions – and four Ballades, which are the most substantial
single-movement pieces he wrote. The rest are the short pieces of
which he was the master.

Chopin – A Middlebrow Mix

The Polonaise

This stately, processional Polish dance becomes in Chopin's
hands a symbol of national heroism and chivalry. The most famous of the polonaises are the 'Miltary in A', (Opus 40), and the
'Heroic in A Flat', (Opus 53).

The Mazurka

This uniquely Polish dance was refined and personalised by Chopin. There are 57 of them, of which a Polish pianist wrote:

> *This is our blood. We are up, down, volcanic – we have*
> *spleen, nostalgia.*

They are all quite short and it's hard to recommend one above all others – so why not listen to a selection and make a personal choice?

The Nocturne

A nocturne is a piece of dreamlike, melodic night music. The credit for inventing the nocturne goes to Irishman John Field, but Chopin grappled it to his soul. The most popular one of all is 'Nocturne in E Flat', (Opus 9, No. 3).

The Waltz

Chopin once declared that "the Viennese waltz is not for me". Instead, he transplanted the waltz from the ballrooms into the salons of the aristocracy and made it more refined and expressive. The 'Waltz in C Sharp Minor' (Opus 64, No. 2) is one of the greatest and the 'Minute Waltz' (Opus 64, No.1) the most celebrated, though it has suffered at the hands of would-be virtuosos trying to get through it in less than 60 seconds. This one is sometimes also known as the 'Dog' waltz, because to Georges Sand it brought to mind a dog chasing its tail.

The Étude

In Chopin's hands, this is no study designed to improve a student's technique. The Études are little works of art, the famous one in E having been described as "the ultimate expression of tender, love-sick longing". In complete contrast is the 'Revolutionary', which we've already mentioned.

The Prelude

Again, the term is not to be taken literally. These are not introductions to anything, but rhapsodic gems in their own right. Of the 24 preludes in Opus 24, the most familiar are 'No. 4 in E Minor' and 'No. 15 in D Flat' (the 'Raindrop').

ROBERT SCHUMANN
(1810-1856)

Schumann has been much in my thoughts recently as I have been doing a two-person play in the USA which featured the great song cycle *Dichterliebe* ('The Poet's Love). My character was a Viennese music professor who needed to play the accompaniments to six or seven of the wonderful songs. It wasn't easy, but playing those pieces was one of the most rewarding things I have ever done in the theatre.

The German Robert Schumann is often confused with the Austrian Franz Schubert, and they do have more in common than sound-alike names. They lived at the same time, both were Romantics, both wrote symphonies and chamber music and were, like Chopin, "poets of the piano". Above all they specialised in the Lieder, which are more than just poems set to music. Each one is a little work of art, achieving a unity of voice, poetry and piano accompaniment.

Schumann first studied law to please his mother, but he always had his own sights set on a musical career and at the age of nineteen he went to study piano with the famed teacher Friedrich Wieck. He straight away fell in love with Wieck's daughter Clara. Papa was outraged and did everything he could to break up the affair, even going so far as to take Schumann to court on the charge that he was a habitual drunk. He sent copies of the charges to Schumann's friends and colleagues, among them Felix Mendelssohn. The drinking charges, though probably having a grain of truth, were later dropped for lack of proof and Schumann finally married his beloved Clara, ten years his junior. She was one of the outstanding pianists of her time and spent many months of each year on tour. Schumann always seemed to be at a low ebb during her absences, but each return and her presence at home inspired him to great heights. Most of his greatest works were written either for Clara or under her inspiration. Schumann had had ambitions to be a concert pianist himself but, while trying to strengthen his fourth finger with a contraption of his own invention, he damaged it beyond repair. That put paid to his piano playing.

Schumann seemed to concentrate on one musical form at a time. Most of his brilliant piano pieces were composed before he was 30, though the 'A Minor Concerto' did come later. The year of his marriage, 1840, was dedicated to writing songs; 1841 was symphony year; 1842 was for chamber music and in 1843 he ventured into the choral field.

In spite of his great love for Clara, who gave him five children and all the inspiration any artist could hope for, the difficult courtship, legal battles and long partings had taken their toll. Schumann began to suffer nervous disorders in the 1840s. Severe bouts of depression progressed into hallucinations in which "demons chanted and angels sang". Even the presence of Brahms, who had become the Schumanns' devoted friend, could not prevent the deterioration. In 1854 Schumann took a despairing leap from a bridge into the Rhine. He was hauled out before drowning, but was committed to a mental institution where he died after another two years of suffering.

Schumann – A Middlebrow Mix

Symphony No. 1 (the 'Spring')

Schumann wrote his first symphony in a single month in a rush of inspiration shortly after his marriage, "In the first flush of spring," he said, "which carries a man away even in his old age." (He had attained the ripe old age of 31!) Having concentrated on piano composition for his first 30 years, Schumann wrote:

> *I am tempted to smash my piano as it is becoming too narrow to contain my ideas. I really have very little practical experience of writing for the orchestra, but I don't despair of acquiring it.*

Well! He doesn't seem to have had too much trouble as he also wrote, when the 'Spring' was nearly finished, that:

> *The symphony has given me many happy hours. I give thanks to the beneficent spirit for allowing me to accomplish a work of such importance in so little time and with such facility.*

This symphony may not be considered Schumann's greatest, but I have no hesitation in giving it the middlebrow vote. Like Mendelssohn's 'Italian' symphony, you know from the opening

bars that you are in for a joyous experience and the energy seldom flags except in the song-like slow movement. Schumann
himself left us notes on the symphony. He said that in the first
movement he meant to "assemble everything that belongs to
Spring – the sprouting green of trees, even the fluttering of butterflies". The finale is fast-moving, dance-like, but Schumann
wrote a cautionary note:

> *I should like to think of it as Spring's farewell – not to be*
> *rendered frivolously!*

Piano Concerto in A Minor (Opus 54)

This is Schumann's most-recorded composition and one of the
most popular of all piano concertos. Strangely, it didn't start life
as a concerto but as a one-movement piece which he called a
'Fantasia'. He wrote it for his beloved Clara in the second year
of their marriage (1841) and it has the same sunny happiness as
the 'Spring' symphony. Miraculously, he seemed to be able to
pick up the inspiration again four years later, when he added a
wistful slow movement and a bright finale and – hey presto! – it
was a concerto.

Clara's first performance was not greeted with unanimous
acclaim. One critic praised her "loyal but futile efforts to make
her husband's curious rhapsody pass for music". Hey ho!

Piano Music

Schumann said that Franz Schubert stood alone as a composer
of piano music, but he probably should have added "0myself
excepted". Of all his piano music I will just recommend the
middlebrow musts.

Carnaval (Opus 9)

This is a 21-movement masterpiece – one biographer said that it
was the first piece in which Schumann "gave his genius full rein".
It is a musical picture of a costume ball whose guests include the
lovers Harlequin and Columbine, and such musical personalities
as Chopin and Paganini. The ball is disrupted by troublemakers,
but all its exotic characters get together to eject them and the piece
ends in a triumphant march. The music has been orchestrated for
a ballet with much the same story.

Kinderscenen ('Scenes from Childhood')

Schumann wrote a lot of pieces for children (some easy ones for his own to play) but this is my favourite set. There are 13 pieces, starting with 'From Foreign Lands'. I play this every time I sit down at a piano as it's the only piece I am confident of playing flawlessly! It was also the opening music for the production *Old Wicked Songs* in which I played a piano teacher. The most famous of the scenes is probably 'Traümerei' ('Dreaming'), which has been much-arranged but is best on piano.

Dichterliebe ('The Poet's Love')

With this song cycle Schumann is considered to be at least the equal of Schubert as a composer of Lieder. There are twenty songs, no doubt inspired again by Clara but dedicated to a celebrated singer of the time. The verses are by Heinrich Heine and Schumann's recurring themes of abandonment and isolation are apparent throughout. The poet goes through all the emotions engendered by unrequited love (ecstasy, jealousy, depression) and in the final piano epilogue, "a glimmer of hope that this experience has not completely destroyed his life" (a quotation from the play *Old Wicked Songs*).

Two of the most famous songs in the cycle are 'Im Wunderschönen Monat Mai ('In the Wondrously Beautiful Month of May') and 'Ich Grolle Nicht' ('I Bear No Grudge').

OTHER EARLY ROMANTIC NOTEWORTHIES

John Field
(1782-1837)

One of the few Irish composers already assured of a place in musical history is John Field. He was a Dubliner and the son of a theatre musician who started to learn the piano at an early age. Before he was ten, young John performed a concerto by Giordani under the composer's direction. Two years later he made his debut in London and took piano lessons there from Clementi, paying for them by serving as a demonstrator in Clementi's piano showrooms. In 1802, when he was twenty, Field accompanied Clementi to Paris, Germany and finally Russia, where he decided to settle. He enjoyed great success as a soloist for 30 years or so but then things began to go wrong for him. His intemperate habits over the years began to take their toll, he could no longer captivate an audience, and he went into a bad decline for the last three or four years of his life.

As a composer Field is, of course, best known for his nocturnes – he is credited with inventing the form which Chopin made so famous. It is not fair, though, that the nocturnes are chiefly remembered for the influence they had on Chopin. They are delicate little gems in their own right, lyrical and reflective. It seems that Field's own playing was characterised by the most perfect legato playing with a singing tone and delicate shades of expression. That is what a pianist needs to give a good account of these pieces today and we have Irish pianists aplenty who have done them justice in recordings. Veronica McSwiney, John O'Conor and Miceal O'Rourke come to mind. Paris-based Miceal O'Rourke also specialises in the Field concertos. There are seven of them, which were heard everywhere in the composer's time and which were later greatly praised by Schumann.

Niccolo Paganini
(1782-1840)

Paganini was one of the most colourful characters in all musical history. He was born in Genoa in 1782 and soon showed an amazing natural talent for the violin. The stories of his technical feats invested his person with something approaching the supernatural. In fact, he himself rather encouraged the idea that he was in league with the devil, though this didn't go down too well with the Church, which for five years after his death refused his body burial in consecrated ground. It was eventually laid to rest in a village graveyard on his own Italian estate. His compositions were designed to display his own incredible technique. Consequently there aren't many violinists who can do them justice.

Paganini invented effects and tricks on the violin which were formerly considered impossible. He revolutionised violin-playing but I often think it was a mistake for later violinists to try to emulate his pyrotechnics. Works like the Mendelssohn and Bruch concertos are the best loved because they are 'violinistic', not calling on the soloist to do anything extraordinary but letting the violin sing like a human voice.

As a composer Paganini has not on the whole been highly rated in spite of implied tributes by Schumann, Liszt, Brahms and Rachmaninov, who based compositions on the notorious Capricci ('caprices') for unaccompanied violin. The two concertos are well worth a listen, both having tuneful final movements. 'Concerto No. 2 in B Minor' is the one known as 'La Campanella' because of the bell-like finale, and this is where Liszt got the idea for his famous piano piece.

Giacomo Meyerbeer
(1791-1864)

The family of Giacomo Meyerbeer resembled that of Mendelssohn – a wealthy German-Jewish business family. Meyerbeer settled in Paris and was at the forefront of operatic life there in the mid-19th century. He went in for big extravaganzas, which flourished in Paris at the time. One of his spectacular works was *Le Prophète*, but the prophet of the title was not of the Old Testament. The story is about a Dutchman in the 16th century who has a strong likeness to King David and is proclaimed a prophet. For sheer grandiose magnificence the coronation scene, with its well-known march, has scarcely ever been rivalled.

Adolphe Adam
(1803-1856)

Adam was a very well-known figure in Parisian music circles in the first half of the 19th century. He was at one time or another a critic, an organist, a conductor and a teacher. He also enjoyed some great success with his operettas – about 40 of them in all. His popularity spread to other European capitals and we remember him best for the full-length ballet *Giselle*, his acknowledged masterpiece and one of the most popular of all Romantic ballets.

Giselle is a peasant girl who falls in love with Count Albrecht, thinking that he is a villager named Loys. When she discovers his true identity and that he is due to marry Countess Bathilde she becomes distraught and kills herself. In Act II the Wilis (dark spirits of the night) draw Giselle from the grave and her spirit appears to Albrecht in the forest. Her love redeems her and releases her from the power of the sinister Wilis. She returns at peace to her grave while Albrecht (who, of course, had loved her all along) is left sorrowing and alone.

The very tuneful overture to the comic opera *If I Were King* is a middlebrow must. Adam's most often-heard piece is the song 'O Holy Night', with Leontyne Price getting the vote over all other singers who have recorded it. In the 1930s several French bishops banned 'O Holy Night' from their churches on the grounds that it wasn't sufficiently religious in spirit, but these days no Christmas would be complete without it.

Mikhail Glinka
(1804-1857)

Mikhail Ivanovich Glinka has an Irish connection, though a slender one – he received a few piano lessons in St Petersburg from the Irish composer John Field. His fame rests mainly on his operas, the first of which was *A Life for the Tsar*. It has a typical Russian folk hero, a full quota of patriotic sentiment and fresh, spontaneous music. It marked a new departure, the birth of a genuinely Russian school of music, and earned for Glinka the title of Prophet Patriarch of Russian Music.

His second opera, *Russlan and Ludmilla*, is based on a fanciful poem by the Russian poet Pushkin, and this opera is regarded as having laid the foundation of a true Russian national style. However, it was not such a great success as its predecessor. It is set in pagan Russia and deals with the tribulations of the Princess Ludmilla who, kidnapped by the magician Chernomor, is finally rescued by one of her three suitors, Russlan, whom she weds.

Glinka wrote this opera in a mood of depression after his separation from his wife, though no-one would guess his state of mind from the overture, which bursts forth effervescently in a Russian folk dance and proceeds with other zestful melodies from the opera. The most enjoyable performance of this overture I have ever heard came from the Irish Youth Orchestra, whose concerts are always inspiring performances.

Otto Nicolai
(1810-1849)

The German composer Nicolai is mainly known through his opera *The Merry Wives of Windsor*, based on Shakespeare's play. It
was first produced in Berlin in 1849 with brilliant success, which
Nicolai did not live to enjoy as he died two months later. *The
Merry Wives of Windsor* still holds its place in German-speaking
countries as one of the most popular of comic operas, with the
overture often being played as a concert piece.

Nicolai was the first conductor of the great Vienna Philhar-
monic Orchestra, which gave its première concert in Vienna in
1842, and that is probably why his music, particularly this very
popular overture, is still often played by the orchestra. It opens
with a lovely melody (that always prompts me to sing out "Are
ye there Mori-ar-eye-ty?") and proceeds to give us a foretaste of
the merry escapades of Sir John Falstaff and company, remind-
ing us of the wit and humour of the Shakespeare original.

THE MID-ROMANTICS (1850-1880)

FRANZ LISZT
(1811-1886)

Franz Liszt came from a small town in Hungary, but he had his musical training in Vienna where he was taught by Salieri and Czerny (the man who wrote all those studies which plagued piano students). In 1823, when he was twelve, Liszt was already a well-known figure in Vienna's musical life. It is said that Beethoven was so moved by the boy's playing at one of his own concerts that he went on to the platform, lifted the young Liszt in his arms and fondly embraced him.

Four years after that, Liszt's father died. His last words to his son were, "You have a good brain and a good heart — beware of women or they will ruin you." Franz doesn't seem to have paid too much attention to this admonition. It is reliably recorded that in the course of his colourful life he had no fewer than 26 "serious" love affairs. Two of the most serious were with women of nobility who also had a way with words. The Comtesse d'Agoult was a novelist writing under the name Daniel Stern, and Liszt's later love Princess Carolyne von Sayn-Wittgenstein was largely responsible for the preface to his orchestral work *Les Préludes*.

Liszt was perhaps the greatest virtuoso pianist the world has ever known. His technique was legendary, his appearance wild and his presence charismatic. He was the Paganini of the piano. His concert tours took him to all parts of the world, including Ireland. In spite of all his success and adulation, Liszt called a halt to his triumphant concert tours when he was only 35, thereafter playing only in private or for charity. During the next 40 years of his life he devoted himself to composing, teaching and furthering the careers of other composers.

In 1843 he settled in Weimar as court artist and later director of the opera and he made Weimar a mecca for musicians. He presented operas by Berlioz and Weber, but his principal protégé was Wagner, though they were about the same age. Liszt conducted Wagner's neglected *Lohengrin*, *The Flying Dutchman*, and *Tannhäuser* and championed his revolutionary music dramas. The two composers fell out, however, when Wagner was responsible

for the break-up of the marriage of Liszt's daughter Cosima.
Cosima, whose mother was the Comtesse d'Agoult, was married to the pianist and conductor Hans von Bülow, but she later
married Wagner.

It is perhaps strange that it was not with his compositions
for piano that Liszt exerted his greatest influence on music. He
may not have exactly invented the symphonic poem, but he is
credited with developing and perfecting it, and creating the model
for people like Saint-Saëns, who once wrote of Liszt and the symphonic poem:

> *This brilliant and fertile creation will be his best title to glory*
> *with posterity.*

Liszt wrote thirteen symphonic poems – the most famous of
which are *Les Préludes*, *Tasso* and *Mazeppa*.

Perhaps Liszt himself best described his own complex and extraordinary personality in the words "half gypsy, half Franciscan". Such was the paradox of his personality that one side of him was given to religious contemplation while the other craved the company of women, the adulation of his audiences and a life of luxury. In later life he actually took holy orders and was granted the title of Abbé.

In 1886, while on a visit to Bayreuth to his daughter Cosima, Liszt caught bronchitis and died after a short illness. He was buried in Bayreuth with the dramatic ceremony appropriate to a great showman. Flowers were showered into the coffin, people threw themselves sobbing in front of it, some even attempted suicide. Liszt would have loved every minute of it.

Liszt – A Middlebrow Mix

Piano Concerto No. 1

This wasn't a great success when first heard in 1849 – Liszt revived it in 1853 and it has survived to become a brilliant showpiece, as one would expect from the arch-showman. If the soloist doesn't dazzle the audience with pianistic pyrotechnics, then he or she is in the wrong business.

Liszt had the audacity to write this concerto in a single movement and fully expected the criticism which did, indeed, come his way. He was innovative in other ways as well, introducing percussion instruments, particularly a triangle, which were looked on with some contempt at the time. In fact, the notorious critic Eduard Hanslick dubbed the entire work "the triangle concerto". However, it is a great outpouring of emotion in a single movement. With all its runs and flourishes, there are probably more notes in this than in any other concerto. It's not something the fainthearted should attempt.

Hungarian Rhapsodies

The nineteen rhapsodies were written for piano and based on Hungarian gypsy music. Some Hungarian high-ups became upset that the world thought that there was nothing more to "national Hungarian" music than the gypsy melodies. Liszt did arrange some of the rhapsodies for orchestra but he considered them best suited to the piano. There were other orchestrations as well, and the Müller – Berghaus arrangement of 'Hungarian Rhapsody No. 2' – is by far the most popular. Runners-up are probably 'Nos. 9', '12' and '14'. Each of the Hungarian Rhapsodies opens with a slow introduction and continues with a fast dance-like section in the same form as the csárdás, the popular Hungarian folk dance.

Liebestraum ('Love's Dream') No. 3

There are three Liebesträume, written first as songs by Liszt for one of his beloved ladies and then adapted for piano. 'No. 3' has become *the* Liebestraum – one of the best-loved of all piano compositions.

La Campanella (the 'Bell')

This is one of the 'Transcendental Studies', and is based on a violin study by Paganini (who also used the tune as the finale to 'Concerto No. 2'). It's a glittering concert piece – testing not only the power but the dexterity and delicacy of the pianist.

Transcriptions

Nobody but Liszt would have dreamed of arranging Beethoven's symphonies for the piano — or the orchestral music of Berlioz and Wagner. The only pianist I ever heard playing the transcriptions was the late Charles Lynch, perhaps the greatest Irish pianist of all time. He had the prodigious technique required – nothing that Liszt wrote would have been any problem to Charles. Liszt also arranged lots of operatic music by Bellini, Donizetti, Verdi and others. It would be well worth while to check out these "concert paraphrases".

RICHARD WAGNER
(1813-1883)

My favourite remark about Wagner is Rossini's, "He has some good moments but some bad quarters of an hour." That about sums up his meaning to middlebrows. None of his operas could be called favourite middlebrow pieces, but there are lots of excerpts, particularly orchestral, which are very popular.

Wagner would not have won any prizes for charm. In fact, he would figure high on any list of the world's most unpleasant men. He was intolerant, unscrupulous, disloyal, immoral – pick your favourite insulting adjective and he was that too. He was convinced that he was a genius and that other people existed largely for his convenience. His genius, of course, cannot be denied but neither can the fact that he was a monster.

Wagner had a passion for the stage from childhood. He studied Shakespeare and Schiller and, at first, his interest was in writing plays – this was something he was able to indulge in throughout his life by writing all his own librettos. He struggled for some time as a young writer of operas but the turning point came in 1839 when he met Meyerbeer, who was producing operas on a grand scale for the Paris Opéra. For a while Meyerbeer was a model and a patron and, under his influence, Wagner composed his first powerful stage dramas – *Lohengrin*, *The Flying Dutchman*, and *Tannhäuser*. Then he went on to conceive *The Ring of the Niebelung*, based on the heroic legends of Germany. This mammoth music drama (the most gigantic work in the history of music) is actually a cycle of four dramas. It took 28 years to write, rewrite, rehearse and finally perform in its entirety at the first Bayreuth Festival in 1876. The total running time is about sixteen hours and the idea is to stretch it out over four days.

A lady called Wilhelmine Planer had the misfortune to marry Wagner in 1836. She found his artistic eminence small compensation for deprivation, insecurity and his excesses and open infidelities. Wagner finally left her and set up house with Cosima, daughter of Franz Liszt and former wife of the conductor Hans von Bülow. In the meantime he had an affair with Mathilde Wesendonck in recognition of the fact that her husband had been helpful and hospitable to him. Wagner's feelings for Mathilde inspired the music drama *Tristan und Isolde* – one of the mightiest of all love stories and he also wrote the five Wesendonck songs for her.

Wagner's life became less tempestuous in later years. One big problem had been that, wherever he was, he always had debtors hammering at his door. In 1864 he met the eighteen-year-old King Ludwig II of Bavaria who fell under his spell and appointed him Royal Director of Music in Munich. Wagner was now guaranteed a steady income and was thus enabled to work steadily towards completing *The Ring Cycle*. He also put his energies into building a theatre at Bayreuth specifically for the purpose of producing *The Ring Cycle* in ideal conditions. I had the good fortune to see a production of *Die Meistersinger* at the Festspielhaus in Bayreuth when I was a student. I also saw dress rehearsals of *Parsifal* and *Tristan und Isolde*. I was at the University of Munich and wrote to Wieland Wagner, grand-nephew of the great man, asking if I could attend. He wrote back giving the

OK, so off I went and it was a memorable experience. The acoustics are reputed to be the best of any opera house in the world. I heard two legendary Wagnerian singers there – Wolfgang Windgassen and Birgit Nillsson – whose voices were of such magnitude that they were in no danger of being submerged in the huge orchestral sound.

Wagner exerted enormous influence on the music world in the second half of the 19th century. Not only did he revolutionise opera, but he was a master of orchestral writing and among his disciples were Richard Strauss, Bruckner and Mahler. He died of a heart attack in Vienna at the age of 69, leaving many people to share his own opinion of himself – that he was the greatest composer in the history of stage music.

Wagner – A Middlebrow Mix

Wagner composed 13 operas – or music-dramas, as they came to be known. There are other works (an early symphony, an oratorio and a piano sonata, for example) but all pale into insignificance compared with the mammoth dramatic works. The big innovation was the dominant rôle given to the orchestra. Wagner developed the leitmotif idea started by Weber. This involves having the main characters, locales, situations or recurrent ideas represented by a short theme which is varied according to the dramatic requirements. "Every bar of dramatic music," Wagner wrote, "is justified only by the fact that it explains something in the action or in the character of the actor."

I think that the best way for middlebrows to approach Wagner is through highlights or excerpts – particularly orchestral. If you enjoy these, you might then decide to chance some "quarters of an hour".

Tannhäuser

This was Wagner's fifth opera and was first produced in Dresden in 1845. Typically, the composer provided his own libretto based on medieval legend. The principal character is a 13th century German knight and minstrel who, in recklessly singing the praises of the love he has known with the immortal goddess Venus, shocks not only his fellow minstrels but also Elizabeth, the pure maiden who loves him.

The most popular number in *Tannhäuser* is the chorus sung by the pilgrims in Act III as they return from Rome and the tune of this great chorus is also featured in the overture.

Lohengrin

This was first produced by Franz Liszt in Weimar in 1850. The action takes place in the 10th century at the court of King Henry I of Saxony. *Lohengrin* is a strange knight who arrives on a boat drawn by a swan, and his marriage to Elsa gives rise to the famous 'Here comes the Bride' march. I can only hope that all the multitudinous marriages launched by this march have been happier than the original – Elsa is poisoned and Lohengrin takes the next swan back to the Holy Grail and the castle of his father Parsifal. Another Wagner must is the prelude to Act III – a stirring piece expressing the whirlwind and joyous wedding preparations and leading into the gentle 'Bridal Chorus'.

Die Walküre (the 'Valkyrie')

This is one of the operas in *The Ring of the Niebelung*, known as *The Ring Cycle*. There is one orchestral piece which is definitely a must – the 'Ride of the Valkyries'. The Valkyries are warrior maidens and the daughters of the mighty god Wotan. The piece depicts their exhilarating horseback ride through the skies as they carry the bodies of dead heroes to Valhalla, the mead-hall of the gods.

Other Wagner Must-Hears

Other Wagnerian orchestral pieces well worthy of your attention are: the preludes to Acts I and III of *Tristan and Isolde*; the prelude to Act I of *Parsifal* (this also has the sublime Good Friday music which you might try later); the overture to *The Flying Dutchman* and the overture and prelude to Act III of *The Mastersingers of Nuremberg*. In fact, *The Mastersingers* is probably the most accessible of all Wagner's operas. It is a comedy centred on a 16th century song contest which is won, of course, by the hero-knight who wins the girl in the process. His prize song is a beauty and there is more pleasant, even-tempered music here than in any of Wagner's other works. If you feel ready to tackle a complete Wagner opera, this is definitely the one to go for.

GIUSEPPE VERDI
(1813-1901)

Verdi sometimes reminds me of Fred Astaire who, when he first went to Hollywood, was judged: "Can't sing, can't act, can dance a bit." The verdict on Giuseppe at the Milan Conservatory was: "Lacking in musical talent"! He nonetheless went on to become one of the greatest operatic specialists, his only real rival being Wagner, who was born in the same year.

Verdi was born in a village in the province of Parma. His father, the local innkeeper and grocer, sent him to live with a cobbler's family in nearby Busseto where he studied the organ. Further studies were made possible by a patron called Antonio Barezzi, whose daughter Verdi married.

Verdi's first opera, *Oberto*, was quite successful and his future looked rosy, but then tragedy struck when his wife and two babies died from an undiagnosed malady. Verdi forced himself to complete a commissioned opera, but it was a failure and he vowed never to write another. However, temptation was put in his way when he was asked to read the story of Nebuchadnezzar. He couldn't resist this biblical story of the King of Babylon and a nation's longing to be delivered from foreign oppression (Italy at the time was under the heel of Austria).

Within a year the opera *Nabucco* was premièred at La Scala to tumultuous acclaim and Verdi was on the road to immortality. For the next eleven years he wrote an opera every nine months or so and his "children" made him a fortune. They included *La Traviata*, *Il Trovatore* and *Rigoletto*. These in particular travelled the world and every Verdi première was a glittering social and musical occasion.

After his "years in the galley", as he called them, Verdi settled back on his peaceful farm but, unlike Rossini, there was much more to come. He was 56 when he wrote *Aida* to celebrate the opening of the Suez Canal and 60 or so when he wrote the thrilling *Requiem*. He also spent five years as a member of parliament after Italy won itself self-government from Austria.

Verdi did marry again and, in memory of his second wife, he founded in Milan a home for impoverished elderly musicians, which still exists. When he died in 1901 a nation mourned. Schools were closed and the Italian Senate was called into special session.

He was indeed, as Tchaikovsky said with a certain gift for understatement, "a very gifted man".

Verdi – A Middlebrow Mix

There may be some pretenders to the throne (Puccini is the only serious one, though), but Verdi is the king of Italian opera. Of the 26 he wrote, the four that get the middlebrow vote are *Rigoletto*, *Il Trovatore* and *La Traviata*, all composed when he was fortyish, and *Aida*, which came about twenty years later.

Rigoletto

This was the opera that turned Verdi from a star into a superstar. Its première in Venice in 1851 was a triumph in more ways than one. The public adored it, but it also marked a victory for Verdi over the censors, who would have put any of their Irish counterparts into the halfpenny place. They shot down the first draft as being "rampant with the most repulsive kind of immorality and obscene vulgarity". However, changes were made which satisfied them and the composer.

The libretto was based on a novel by Victor Hugo and one clever ruse was in switching the action from the French Court of François I to that of an anonymous Duke in 16th century Italy. He is a wicked Duke who seduces the daughter (Gilda) of his deformed jester Rigoletto. In reprisal, Rigoletto hires the bandit Sparafucile to kill the Duke. Maddalena, Sparafucile's sister, falls for the Duke and begs her brother to spare him. Sparafucile agrees to murder instead the first person to enter the inn. Gilda overhears this and sacrifices herself. When Rigoletto retrieves a sack from Sparafucile, the corpse turns out to be that of his daughter instead of the Duke, fulfilling a curse placed on Rigoletto by a courtier who had been ridiculed by him.

The jester is a wonderful rôle for a baritone. The best I ever saw was Piero Cappucilli in the Gaiety Theatre in Dublin many years ago. His acting was almost on a par with his singing, which made the great Act I monologue ('Pari siamo') and his other outpourings both moving and memorable. The unsavoury Duke is given some of the tastiest tunes. 'La Donna è mobile' ('Woman is fickle') is among the most popular of all tenor arias and 'Questa o quella' is another gem. Gilda's big aria is 'Caro nome' ('Dear name') a coloratura showpiece for soprano. Then there is the Act III quartet 'Bella figlia dell'amore', one of the most celebrated of all ensemble numbers: inside the inn where the murder is to take place, the Duke lightheartedly makes love to Maddalena while outside Gilda despairingly observes her lover's faithlessness and Rigoletto assures her that she will be avenged.

Il Trovatore

It took Verdi only 28 days to write the music of this great opera. It has been described as "a tragedy that runs the gamut of sorcery, burning at the stake, death by axe, poison and sword". On this point Verdi himself remarked:

> *Some people say the opera is too sad and there are too many deaths. But in life all is death.*

A gloomy outlook indeed, but the gory plot is retrieved by magnificent melodies.

The success of the première in 1853 surpassed even that of *Rigoletto,* and the speed with which it swept the world was even more sensational. The opera is set in 15th-century Spain and the plot centres on the beautiful Countess Leonora, the young troubadour Manrico with whom she is in love and the Count di Luna who loves her. The Count does not know that Manrico is in fact his younger brother, believed to have been killed in infancy by the gypsy woman Azucena. She has brought Manrico up as her own son. They are both thrown into prison by the Count and Azucena is forced to watch as Manrico is executed. Leonora dies too, having taken poison, but not before revealing to the Count that he has killed his own brother.

Il Trovatore probably has more well-loved numbers than any other opera: 'Stride la vampa' is Azucena's account of how her mother was burned at the stake; 'Il balen del suo sorriso' is Count di Luna's declaration of love for Leonora; 'Di quella pira' is the thrilling tenor aria in which Manrico exhorts his men to rescue Azucena. Then there is the famous 'Miserere' chanted by the monks while above it Leonora and Manrico sing their farewell duet. 'Home to our mountains' is the duet in which Manrico and Azucena express their longing to return home. Is there any end to this? Well! Not before mentioning the soldiers' chorus and the ultra popular 'Anvil' chorus, sung by the gypsies as they hammer away at their anvils in their encampment at the foot of the mountains.

La Traviata

Verdi's opera *La Traviata* was based on the novel *The Lady of the Camelias* by Alexandre Dumas (famous, of course, for *The Three Musketeers*). The opera was an utter failure at its first performance and was almost laughed off the stage at one point in the final scene. When the soprano in the rôle of Violetta, a lady of enormous proportions, was supposed to be on the point of death from consumption, the audience fell about. When the work was introduced to London three years later *The Times* critic railed at "the representation of all that is foul and hideous in human nature". But as Verdi himself said, "Was the fault mine or the singers? Time will tell." The years have indeed given their answer. *La Traviata* is one of the most popular of all operas and is packed with musical delights.

Set in Paris and its surrounds in about 1850, Alfredo Germont falls in love with the notorious courtesan Violetta. They live happily together in the country for a while until Alfredo's father persuades Violetta to end the liaison for the good of the Germont name. She returns to Paris and resumes her former life. Alfredo, misunderstanding her motives, insults her, but before she dies from her fatal illness, they are reunited in love and allow themselves to dream of a happy future.

La Traviata is also chock-full of marvellous numbers. In Act I there is the famous drinking song 'Libiamo' and the soprano aria 'Ah! Fors é lui' in which Violetta dreams of the possibility of true love. Act II has one of the loveliest of all baritone arias, 'Di provenza il mar', in which old Germont tries to comfort his son; in Act III Violetta has the aria 'Addio, del passato', realising that she has only God's mercy to depend on. The final lovers' duet 'Parigi o cara' is also memorable. Orchestrally, the preludes to Acts I and III are exquisite but often criminally ignored by insensitive late-comers or bar-lingerers.

Aida

Aida was commissioned for the Italian opera house in Cairo and had its first performance there in 1871. It's set in Egypt at the time of the Pharaohs and has all the appeal of a great pageant. Six weeks after its Cairo première it was presented at La Scala, Milan, with Verdi conducting. It is reported that:

> *He was recalled 32 times and presented with an ivory baton and diamond star with the name of* Aida *done in rubies and his own in other precious stones.*

Things were done in style in those days.

The plot centres on the love of the Egyptian warrior Radames for the captive Ethiopian Princess Aida and the jealousy of Amneris, daughter of the King of Egypt. Radames unwittingly commits treason and is condemned to be buried alive, but Aida has concealed herself in the vault and they die in each other's arms. I always feel sorry for the tenor, who has to sing the huge aria 'Celeste Aida' almost as soon as he opens his mouth – prior warming-up is essential. Also in Act I Aida sings 'Ritorna vincitor' ('Return victorious') – she is torn between her love for Radames and love of her Ethiopian homeland. The most spectacular scene in the opera is the triumphant return of the Egyptians from war – we hear the chorus 'Glory to Egypt', the celebrated triumphal march and then the exotic ballabile or ballet music.

I saw *Aida* in Vienna when I was a student, with Leontyne Price in the title role and Herbert von Karajan conducting. It was a wondrous spectacle in what was then (and perhaps still is) the most advanced opera house in Europe. There were horses and elephants – you name it! Duffy's Circus with the most marvellous music attached. It's one of my great memories.

CHARLES GOUNOD
(1818-1893)

Charles Gounod would not generally be regarded as one of the world's greatest composers, but he has enough middlebrow music to his credit to get him into the Top 40.

He was the son of an artist and a musician and went the way of most French composers, studying at the Conservatoire de Paris and winning the Prix de Rome. He was only twenty when he went to Italy and the Italian culture, particularly Italian religious culture, had a profound influence on him. He actually studied for the priesthood but was dissuaded by worldly friends (one of them was Mendelssohn's favourite sister Fanny) from pursuing this course. Throughout his life he maintained an interest in the sacred and religious that is evident in all his masses and oratorios.

Gounod spent five years in London as a refugee from the Franco-Prussian war and had marital problems as well as disputes with the Opéra Comique in Paris. Of all his operas, the only one to have remained in the repertoire is the enormously popular *Faust*. Gounod died, blind and paralysed, at the age of 75, the last years of his life having been largely unfruitful.

Gounod – A Middlebrow Mix

Faust

The first production of Gounod's opera *Faust* was in Paris in 1859, and it met with no great success, though parts of it were singled out for praise. An enterprising publisher, however, decided to take a chance and issue the score, and to his utter surprise it made him a fortune. Consequently, when *Faust* was re-introduced ten years later its success was assured and to this day it has remained one of the best-loved of all operas.

In order to regain his youth, the aged philosopher Faust (tenor) makes a pact with the devil, in the person of Mephistopheles (bass). Now a young nobleman, Faust sets his cap at Marguerite (soprano) and succeeds in seducing her in spite of the efforts of her devoted admirer Liebel (mezzo or tenor), whose flowers cannot match the jewels planted by Mephistopheles on Faust's behalf. Valentin returns from the war to find that his sister Marguerite has given birth to Faust's child and, in an attempt to avenge her honour, he is killed by Faust in a duel and curses his sister for being the cause of his death. Faust abandons Marguerite and heads off to enjoy the revelries of Walpurgis Night, being mesmerised by will-o'-the-wisps and witches and titillated by legendary courtesans of antiquity. He returns to find that the insane Marguerite has killed their infant child and been imprisoned. He seeks to rescue her, but she calls for divine protection which is granted as angels come to transport her soul to heaven – a reprieve which can hardly be expected for himself by the grieving Faust!

Once his opera was accepted for production at the Paris Opéra, Gounod had to come up with some ballet music for it. At first he was reluctant and asked his young friend Saint-Saëns to write it on his behalf but shortly afterwards he changed his mind and wrote it himself. He chose as his subject Faust's experiences on the legendary Walpurgis Night, the eve of May Day. Faust sees parading before him all the *femmes fatales* of classical history – including Helen of Troy and Cleopatra. The music is sensuous, exotic and the Bacchanale makes an exciting climax.

Highlights of the opera include 'Avant de quitter ces lieux' ('Before leaving these places'), the baritone aria in Act II in which Valentin instructs his friend to look after his sister Marguerite during his absence on the battlefield and, of course, the great tenor aria 'Salut demeure chaste et pur' ('All hail thou dwelling pure and lowly') in which Faust hails and praises Marguerite's abode.

Roméo et Juliette

This opera was a success for Gounod in 1867 during the Paris Exhibition. He badly needed it, for *Faust* had been followed by a few failures. The highlight for middlebrows is the lovely waltz song 'Je veux vivre' ('I want to live'). This was written at the request of the diva Marie Miolan-Carvalho late in the rehearsal period and became a big hit.

Other Gounod Must-Hears

For *Ave Maria*, Gounod fitted his lovely melody to a prelude by Bach, fashioning a prayer to the Virgin which vies for popularity with Schubert's. *Judex* is an emotional orchestral interlude from the oratorio *Mors et Vita* ('Death and Life') that has become a popular middlebrow piece.

JACQUES OFFENBACH
(1819 – 1880)

Rossini had something to say about most of the composers he knew, and he called Offenbach "the Mozart of the Champs-Elysées", though "the French Johann Strauss", as he was also called, was probably closer to the mark. He was the son of a Jewish cantor and was born in the little town of Offenbach, near Cologne.

He settled in Paris at an early stage in his career and decided to adopt the name of his home town – thus Jakob Eberst became Jacques Offenbach. He became more French than the French, both in his personality and his style of writing. After a short spell of studying at the Paris Conservatoire, he got a job as a cellist in the orchestra of the Opéra Comique. He also gave solo recitals, being acclaimed by no less a personage than the young Queen Victoria. He went from the Opéra Comique to the Comédie Française as conductor of the orchestra, a job that entailed conducting a great deal of incidental music and songs, much of which he composed himself. All this theatre experience was invaluable, but he became dissatisfied because he was now writing his own one-act comedies and couldn't get them staged. Eventually he left and formed his own company in a rickety little theatre off the Champs-Elysées which he called the Bouffes Parisiens. ('Bouffes' was a word of his own invention, a mixture of opera buffa – Italian comic opera – and 'ouf!' – the unique, untranslatable sound French people make when they can't think of a suitable comment.)

Things went so well at the Bouffes that Offenbach was soon able to move to better premises. He produced a succession of operettas which became immensely popular – they were witty comedies, making fun of everything from Greek mythology to French bureaucracy and the pomposity of the Parisian officials. Above all, they were crammed with melodious, infectious music which made them irresistible. His operettas were popular outside Paris too, on tours of the Bouffes company to the French provinces and also to London and Vienna. On one trip to Vienna Offenbach encouraged Johann Strauss Jr to enter the operetta field – telling him that he was far too talented to just write polkas and waltzes. In London he had an influence on Arthur Sullivan, who set aside his lofty ambitions to become a great composer and instead became the English Offenbach.

Offenbach had his own lofty ambitions and towards the end of his life his one wish was to see the production of the opera on which he had been working for some years and which he hoped would be his highest achievement. This was *The Tales of Hoffman*, but sadly he died before completing it. The version which went on at the Opéra Comique three months later was one that Offenbach might just about have recognised, but it was a big hit and played no fewer than 101 nights in the year of its production.

Offenbach – A Middlebrow Mix

The Tales of Hoffman

This opera got its name because it is based on the famous stories by the German writer E. T. A. Hoffman. In the prologue, the poet Hoffman is carousing with friends in a tavern beside an opera house. He is crazy about Stella, a diva, and in his cups relates the tales of three previous love affairs. There is an act devoted to each and all end tragically. The first is Olympia, a singing doll who can only function when wound up. The next is Antonia, who is so frail that any exertion would kill her. She is urged to sing and duly expires. The last is the courtesan Giulietta, who also leaves Hoffman in the lurch. Back in the tavern we hear that all these fantasy women were personifications of Stella, who arrives in the tavern only to reject the hapless Hoffman.

The Olympia episode has the great soprano showpiece 'Les oiseaux dans la charmille', known as 'The doll's song'. The doll's clockwork mechanism keeps running down and she has to be wound up in order to continue with the brilliant vocal gymnastics. The high spot of the Antonia act is when she endangers her life by singing ('Elle a fui, la tourterelle'). The Giulietta affair is set in Venice and gives us the celebrated Barcarolle ('Belle nuit, o nuit d'amour'). This is often now heard in orchestral versions, but in the opera it is a duet sung by Giulietta and Nicklausse as they drift languorously in a gondola soaking up the romantic atmosphere of Venice by night.

Orpheus in the Underworld

This is one of the great operettas, up there with the best of Strauss or Gilbert and Sullivan. Sometimes known as *To Hell with*

Orpheus, it is a big send-up of the Greek legend of Orpheus and
Eurydice. Instead of being a wonder on the lyre, this Orpheus is
a bad fiddle player. He isn't a bit upset when his flirtatious wife
is bitten by a snake and transported to hell. Eurydice, for her
part, finds the underworld a much more exciting place to be.
She enjoys the attentions of Pluto (ruler of the Underworld) and
the mighty Jupiter, who descends disguised as a fly in order to
get through the keyhole. Orgies are the order of the day. The
only thing that nearly spoils it is when Orpheus reluctantly turns
up to retrieve his wife. As in mythology, he is told that she can
leave as long as he doesn't turn around to see if she is following.
In the operetta, the jealous Jupiter fires a thunderbolt at him
which, not surprisingly, causes him to turn. That makes
everybody happy. Eurydice can stay put, Orpheus can go home
unburdened and the Underworld can can-can in a frenzy of
Bacchanalian merrymaking.

Offenbach wrote *Orpheus in the Underworld* at a time when
he was in serious financial straits. He desperately needed a com-
mercial success in order to keep his creditors at bay. He must
have been a worried man, because the operetta ran into a lot of
first-night problems and was not a huge hit when premièred in
1858. An influential critic, however, did it a great favour by de-
nouncing it as immoral, scandalous, shocking and "a profanity
of holy and glorious antiquity". Naturally, the operetta at once
became the toast of Paris.

There are catchy tunes all the way through, but the 'Can-
can' is indisputably the highlight. Parisians went wild for it and
this uninhibited vaudeville dance became all the rage – the French
hucklebuck! The American writer Mark Twain was impressed
when he visited France:

> *The idea of the can-can is to dance as wildly, as noisily, and*
> *as furiously as you can, to expose yourself as much as possi-*
> *ble if you are a woman and to kick as high as you can, no*
> *matter which sex you belong to.*

Twain went on at much greater length but I wouldn't want you to
become too excited. A lot of the great *Orpheus* tunes are in the
overture – a brilliant pot-pourri put together by Carl Binder for
the first production in Vienna in 1860.

Other operettas by Offenbach which have often found their way into *Music for Middlebrows* are *La Belle Hélène*, *The Grand Duchess of Gerolstein* and *La Vie Parisienne*. They all have sparkling overtures and if you want a sampler of the galops, waltzes, cancans of "the French Johann Strauss" you need look no further than the score of the ballet *Gaieté Parisienne*. The ballet suite is full of the good-humoured, frivolous, tuneful music that made this German the favourite composer of Napoleon III's Second Empire.

BEDRICH SMETANA
(1824-1884)

Bedrich Smetana is the only composer whose music is heard every week on *Music for Middlebrows*. I chose 'Dance of the Comedians' from *The Bartered Bride* as my signature tune because it has an impressive opening, is lively and tuneful and builds up to an exciting climax. I suppose I might have been a little influenced too by my own love of comedy and involvement in it at the time.

Smetana's father was a brewer in a little Bohemian town in the southern Czech Republic, then part of Austria. He encouraged his son's violin and piano playing, for fun, being himself an amateur musician. However, he wasn't enthusiastic about Bedrich becoming a composer and did little to support his musical education. Young Smetana had to support himself and his studies as best he could and he survived by giving lessons. For some time he was music master to the family of Count Thun, which at least assured him of three meals at day. Then at the age of 25, Smetana appealed to the great Franz Liszt for financial help to open a music school in Prague. The two had never met, but Liszt came up trumps. The school was opened with Smetana as director and his pianist wife, whom he had married in 1848, as assistant.

Smetana admired the music of Beethoven, Schumann, Berlioz and especially Liszt, but there was no question as to what kind of music he most wanted – Czech music. He was a patriotic, fervent nationalist and wasn't a bit happy with the heavy-handed Austrian domination of Prague. He had a special place in his heart for the nationalist mazurkas and polonaises of Chopin, who similarly resented the Russian domination of Poland.

In 1856 Smetana accepted a conducting post in Gothenburg, Sweden. Prague was not a comfortable place for him to be at the time, as an attempt to gain Czech independence had failed and he was also mourning the death of his five-year-old daughter. He spent five years in the free and bracing air of Sweden where he did some serious composing. He was very much under the influence of Liszt, whose symphonic poems he much admired and attempted to emulate. In a letter to Liszt he wrote:

> *I cannot describe to you the soul-stirring impression your music has made on me. Art, as taught by you, has become my credo.*

Smetana's wife died during his sojourn in Sweden. He married again, but his second wife, a Bohemian girl, could not acclimatise to the harsh northern climate, and so they packed up and returned to Prague. Here Smetana helped to establish a society dedicated to nationalist music. He became director of the new National Opera House and his own operas, all based on Czech themes, were produced there one after the other. The best known and most successful of these was *The Bartered Bride*.

In 1874, Smetana became totally deaf. Unlike Beethoven, he was not forewarned, the affliction came suddenly after a period of ill health and overwork. As a result his mental health deteriorated and he spent a considerable time in mental institutions, finally dying in one a few months after his 60th birthday.

He is remembered as the father of Czech national music. His compositions are intensely nationalistic, painting Bohemia in all its aspects – its meadows and deep forests, its streams, villages, castles and legendary past. It is often boisterous and plain fun to hear, but can also be poetic and extremely moving.

Smetana – A Middlebrow Mix

Vltava, or The Moldau

This is the most popular of the six symphonic poems in the cycle called 'Ma Vlast' ('My Country'). The cycle depicts landscapes from rural Bohemia and episodes from Bohemian history or folk legend. The 'Moldau' is the second of the series, written when Smetana was already stone deaf. It is a portrait of the river running through the Bohemian countryside and has a magnificent central theme which is very familiar. The composer himself gave us his interpretation, which I have condensed here:

> *Two springs gush in a Bohemian forest and sparkle in the morning sun. The waters unite in a brook which rushes on and becomes a mighty river, the Moldau. It flows through meadows and lowlands where a wedding feast is being joyously celebrated. At night wood and water nymphs hold their revels and castles and fortresses are reflected in the water. The rapids of St John are negotiated and the river flows on in majestic calm towards Prague, finally disappearing from the poet's gaze in the distance.*

The Bartered Bride

This is Smetana's masterpiece – recognised not only as the quintessential Czech national opera but as one of the greatest of all folk operas. It wasn't an immediate success when first performed in 1866, but it didn't then have all those marvellous orchestral dances and Smetana did a lot of tinkering with it before he was finally satisfied.

The action takes place at a village fair in Bohemia and the basic story is about two lovers who survive all sorts of misunderstandings and masquerades en route to their wedding. The opera is chock-full of lively Bohemian-sounding tunes and dances. They sound like real folk music, though Smetana insisted they were all original creations. There are some good tunes for the singers but the best ones are for the orchestra. The overture really sets everything up – it's brisk and jolly and the most famous dances are 'Polka', 'Furiant' and, of course, 'Dance of the Comedians'. This last-named has been the signature tune of *Music for Middlebrows* since the word go. I would venture to suggest that its opening bars are more familiar in Ireland than they are in The Czech Republic.

Other Smetana Must-Hears

'From My Homeland' is the title given to two very tuneful duets for piano and violin. The 'Quartet No. 1 in E Minor' is subtitled 'Out of My Life' and Smetana wrote detailed notes about the aspects of his life depicted in each of the four movements. Even in this chamber work he finds room for a polka in the second movement.

JOHANN STRAUSS JR
(1825-1899)

There were at least half a dozen Strausses working in the music business in Vienna through the 19th century. Johann Sr was the patriarch and the others were his sons and nephews. Senior fathered six children with his wife and five with a mistress. The Strausses ran a successful dance orchestra which toured the world playing waltzes, galops and polkas composed by family members. They also ran a music-publishing business and made a fortune from sheet music sales. However, it wasn't one big happy family. Strauss Sr wanted all the glory for himself and discouraged his sons from following in his musical footsteps. Johann Jr wasn't to be denied. With his mother's support he sneaked lessons anyhow and in time had much more training than his father.

Johann Sr walked out on his family in 1842 and set up house with his mistress and their progeny. This was probably a relief to Strauss Jr, who was then able to do his own thing without having to suffer his father's jealousies and recriminations at close quarters.

A couple of years later the nineteen-year-old Strauss Jr launched his own orchestra at Dommayer's Casino. Supporters of his father went along to disrupt the proceedings, but didn't manage to dampen the enthusiasm of the audience. Johann Sr didn't last long after this and when he died in 1849 at the age of 45, Strauss Jr took over his band. Merged with his own it became one of the best in Europe, "worth walking to Vienna to hear". Johann recruited his brothers Eduard and Josef to help him out with the conducting, and they all also composed attractive pieces (Josef was a great polka man) which the orchestra played all over the place – indeed, their fame spread to America, where Johann conduced fourteen monster concerts for the American Jubilee in Boston in 1872, as well as four more in New York. It is reported that he received $100,000 for this, which is probably more than Phil Coulter gets nowadays.

In 1871, at the suggestion of Offenbach, Strauss began writing operettas and, for the next fifteen years, no season at the Viennese Theater an der Wien was complete without a new work from him. Not many of them are memorable, however. Towering above them all is *Die Fledermaus* and the runner-up is *The Gypsy Baron*.

Some people look down their nose a bit at Johann Strauss Jr,

but he was a genius admired and even envied by some of the big
guns of the time – Brahms, Wagner, Richard Strauss (no relation), Maurice Ravel and many more. All over the world people
whirled to his waltzes, which captured the spirit of light-hearted
19th century Vienna. He was truly the 'Waltz King', and when he
died in Vienna in 1899, one critic wrote that he was "as assured of
immortality as Beethoven or Brahms".

Strauss – A Middlebrow Mix

The Operettas

It was Jacques Offenbach, it seems, who persuaded Johann Strauss
Jr to turn his attention to writing operettas. Offenbach was visiting Vienna and is supposed to have said to Strauss:

> *Waltzes, charming as they are, are not enough for a man of*
> *your gifts. You must pull yourself together and write for the*
> *stage.*

This may be more fantasy than fact, but at the age of 46 Strauss
did write an operetta and another fifteen or so after that, but the
only real successes were *Die Fledermaus* and *The Gypsy Baron*. He
was already established as the Waltz King, and it wasn't until
1874 that *Die Fledermaus* took the stage.

Die Fledermaus

Die Fledermaus was premièred in 1874, and Vienna could hardly
have been in the mood to receive it. The Stock Exchange had just
collapsed and the country was in a state of economic disaster.
The operetta was withdrawn after only sixteen performances but
when it was staged in Berlin two months later it had the success
it deserved and has been regarded ever since as the epitome of
Viennese operetta. It is performed in all the top opera houses of
the world and has to be seen to be fully appreciated. The plot is
convoluted (as in all the best comic operas) and I can't resist quoting Victor Borge's summary:

> *The main characters in Johann Strauss's operetta Die*
> *Fledermaus are Gabriel von Eisenstein, when he isn't pre-*
> *tending to be the Marquis Renard; Rosalinde, his wife, when*

she isn't pretending to be a Hungarian countess; Adèle, her chambermaid, when she isn't pretending to be Olga the actress; Frosch, the jailer, when he isn't pretending to be the Chevalier Chagrin; and Alfred, the singing teacher, when he isn't pretending to be Gabriel von Eisenstein. The only person who isn't pretending to be someone else is Prince Orlovsky and he's always played by a woman.

It's no wonder that *Die Fledermaus* continues to be popular, because it has all the best of Strauss – waltzes to beat the band, great songs and choruses, catchy tunes. It has lots of laughter too – Frosch, the jailer is often played by a local comedian and given his head and in some productions the singers throw in popular numbers which aren't by Strauss at all. Sets and costumes can also add to the overall effect. I saw a production in Trinidad once which was incredibly colourful and spectacular.

The best known songs are Adele's 'Mein Herr Marquis', popularly known as 'The laughing song' and Rosalinde's csárdás number 'Klänge der heimat' in which she sings of her Magyar homeland. Then there is 'Brüderlein und schwesterlein' in which Dr Falke praises the spirit of brotherly and sisterly love which has come over everyone. There are great choruses too – particularly one in which the librettist excelled himself with words like 'Dui-du, dui-du, hu, hu, hu'.

A lot of the lovely music of *Die Fledermaus* is in the score for the ballet *Graduation Ball*, a recording of this would be well worth the investment. One writer said of Strauss:

He wrote his operettas for the delectation of the masses and for their entertainment; but, because he was a man of genius, what he touched was often transformed into a work of art.

The Gypsy Baron

This was the tenth work by Strauss to be staged. It received its première in Vienna on the eve of the composer's 60th birthday in 1885. I don't think Johann could have wished for any other birthday present than the reception given to his new operetta. It was a sensational success and must have gone on nearly all night because the audience kept insisting on encore after encore. The overture was applauded many times throughout and put the audience into just the right mood for the delights that were to follow.

None of Strauss's other operettas achieved the success of these two but they all had great waltzes, many of which have become popular as separate pieces. The waltz 'Roses from the south', for example, is made up of themes from 'Das Spitzentuch der Königin' ('The Queen's handkerchief').

Waltzes and Other Dances

George Bernard Shaw once said:

> *In art, the highest success is to be the last of your race, not the first. Anybody, almost, can make a beginning. The difficulty is to make an end – to do what cannot be bettered.*

Shaw might well have been thinking of Strauss Jr, who didn't invent the waltz, but who brought it to perfection as an art form. He developed it in such a way that it became a tone picture not only of his beloved Vienna but of the whole golden age in which he lived – the era of the Emperor Franz Josef.

The most famous waltz of all is, of course, *The Blue Danube*. Brahms once jotted down a few bars of it and added: " Not, unfortunately, by Johannes Brahms." It was written as a choral waltz in 1867 for the Viennese Men's Choral Society. Like all Strauss's finest waltzes, it is not so much a single dance movement as a continuous suite of waltzes with an introduction and a rousing conclusion. One biographer has written:

> *The universe of the waltz can be epitomised in about fifteen minutes simply by playing* The Blue Danube. *More eloquently, more concisely than any other work, it embodies the essence of the waltz in form and spirit. The music takes subtle hold of the listener and makes him a living part of a vanished world.*

Other waltzes which are definitely musts include 'Tales from the Vienna Woods', 'Wine, women, and song', 'Artist's life', 'The Emperor Waltz' and 'Wiener Blut' ('Vienna Spirit').

Some of the most popular polkas are 'Thunder and lightning', 'Tritsch-tratsch' and 'Pizzicato' (brother Eduard had a part in this), while brother Josef contributed the marvellous 'Feuerfest' ('Firebell') polka and Johann Sr gets the credit for the 'Radetzsky' march without which no concert of Strauss music would be complete. This march was composed in honour of a remarkable old Field Marshall who was still sitting up straight as a ramrod on his horse at the age of 82. The piece became a symbol of the military might of the old Hapsburg monarchy.

JOHANNES BRAHMS
(1833-1897)

Brahms is the third of the three Bs so often mentioned in 'music appreciation'. He worshipped the other two: Bach and Beethoven. In fact, he was so much in awe of Beethoven as a symphonist that he considered himself unworthy to follow in the master's footsteps. For nearly sixteen years Brahms let his first symphony germinate in his mind. He was 43 when he eventually considered it finished and let it be heard. Ironically, it was hailed by some as the "Beethoven Tenth".

Brahms spent his childhood in the slums of Hamburg. His father, a double-bass player, was far from affluent, but somehow managed to ensure that Johannes received a sound musical education. The young man was also able to earn a bit himself by playing the piano in bars and brothels. When he was twenty, Brahms toured with the Hungarian violinist Eduard Reményi and this partnership had a big impact on his life. It stimulated his interest in Hungarian gypsy music, which led to his composing the hugely popular 'Hungarian Dances'. It also gave him the opportunity of meeting the great violinist Joseph Joachim, who gave him letters of introduction to Liszt in Weimar and Schumann in Düsseldorf.

His visit to Liszt was not a great success – perhaps because he fell asleep when Liszt was playing the piano for the entertainment of guests in his house. However, Brahms struck up an immediate rapport with Schumann and his pianist wife Clara. Schumann hailed Brahms as the genius the musical world had long been waiting for and his career was assured.

Brahms became close friends with the Schumanns and was a great comfort to Clara during her husband's distressing illness and his death not long afterwards. In fact, Brahms was probably in love with Clara, though she was fourteen years his senior and they carried on a long correspondence. Brahms never married, though there were other women in his life and his early experiences on the docks in Hamburg perhaps helped him later in life to be comfortable in the company of ladies of the night.

Though a late starter on symphonies, Brahms, by his early forties, was one of the most respected composers in Europe. He had legions of admirers and devotees who called themselves the

Brahmins. They championed his mellow music, claiming that he stood for true musical values in an art corrupted by experimenters like Wagner. Brahms himself was outspoken in his views on other composers. He was, in fact, outspoken about most things — a story goes that he once left a party saying:

> *If there is anybody here I have not insulted, I apologise.*

He lived a quiet bachelor life in Vienna, avoiding travel whenever possible apart from summer walking holidays in Italy and the Alps. He died of cancer at the age of 63.

Brahms – A Middlebrow Mix

Hungarian Dances

When Brahms came to write his 'Hungarian Dances' he at no time claimed them as original. In fact, he called them "arrangements", and in a letter to his publisher he said:

> *I offer them as genuine gypsy children which I did not beget*
> *but merely brought up with bread and milk.*

Originally piano duets, they were later arranged for orchestra, some by Brahms himself, others by Dvorák or other composers.
   There are 21 dances in all, some of which are hugely popular and are heard in all sorts of arrangements. Perhaps the best known of all is 'Hungarian Dance No. 1'. If you're a film buff you may remember Charlie Chaplin in *The Great Dictator* doing a hilarious shaving scene to this music. Of the arrangements, I would recommend those for violin and piano by the virtuoso Joseph Joachim (Itzhak Perlman does a great job on these, as he does on everything.)

Violin Concerto in D

Most of the great violin concertos have been written with a specific soloist in mind. If the chosen violinist happened to be a brilliant virtuoso, then the work tended to be of extreme technical difficulty. Sometimes, as in the case of Paganini, the designated soloist was the composer himself. This gave great problems to succeeding generations of violinists, as Paganini was able to do things not within the capabilities of ordinary mortals. Brahms was greatly helped in the composition of his violin concerto by Joseph Joachim, one of the most eminent violinists of the 19th century, who was the only one who attempted to play the concerto for a while. Even the great Spaniard Sarasate refused to add it to his repertoire, though he gave as his reason the fact that he "wasn't prepared to stand there as a listener, with his fiddle in his hand, while the oboe played the only melody in the entire work".

The concerto took shape in the summer of 1878. Brahms was in good mood at the time, as his second symphony had just been given a warm reception by the public and he decided to treat himself to a holiday in Italy. The warmth of the Italian sunshine carries over into the piece.

After a full-scale orchestral introduction, the violin enters dramatically but soon gives us a romantic songlike melody. Brahms wrote no cadenza (an unaccompanied show-off piece for a soloist) but left it to Joachim to provide one, which has since been used by most soloists. Then, at the beginning of the second movement, comes that charming pastoral melody voiced by the oboe, while the soloist waits impatiently to get at it. When the violin is allowed to enter, it does not repeat the tune but embroiders it and rhapsodises on it. The finale is a brilliant rondo in the Hungarian style so beloved of Johannes Brahms.

Academic Festival Overture

Brahms turned down an offer of an honorary doctorate from Cambridge University, principally because he had to attend in person and he was terrified of the sea. However, he accepted one from Breslau University and composed an overture for the occasion. The assembled dignitaries were shocked to find that it was a pot-pourri of German student songs concluding in grand style with the student anthem 'Gaudeamus Igitur'.

Variations on a Theme of Haydn

This is in fact a misnomer as the theme is the St Anthony Chorale and was not composed by Haydn at all. He just recognised a good tune when he heard it. The variations are wonderful and this is Brahms at his sonorous, orchestral best. There is also a version for two pianos, but the orchestra wins hands down.

Songs

Brahms was a master songwriter, from full-scale Lieder in the Schubert style to little vocal gems like the world-famous Lullaby ('Guten abend, gute nacht') which you undoubtedly know, but for identification purposes it is Opus 49, No. 4.

LÉO DELIBES
(1836-1891)

The appearance of Léo Delibes in the Top 40 may cause some surprise and I will admit that he scrapes in only by a short head. He makes it on the strength of the two ballets *Sylvia* and *Coppélia*, which are great middlebrow favourites and the opera *Lakmé*.

Delibes studied at the Paris Conservatoire, where one of his teachers was Adolphe Adam, the composer of the ballet *Giselle* as well as lots of operas and operettas. Through the influence of Adam, Delibes got a job as accompanist at the Théâtre Lyrique and also as organist at a couple of churches. Ten years later, in 1863, he was appointed Repetiteur at the Paris Opéra. This involved teaching the 100 singers their notes and playing piano for rehearsals – a thankless chore for someone who longed to be a stage composer.

Eventually the chance came his way to show what he could do. Delibes was commissioned to collaborate with the Polish musician Minkus on the ballet *La Source*. He completely eclipsed the experienced Pole with a torrent of melody and was immediately asked to write a divertissement (sequence of dances) to be introduced into the ballet *Le Corsaire* by his old master Adolphe Adam. This in turn led to his first complete ballet *Coppélia*, which broke new ground and undoubtedly exercised an influence on Tchaikovsky.

In addition to ballet music, Delibes wrote lots of operas and operettas which were produced at the Opéra Comique or the Bouffes Parisiens (Offenbach's establishment). We don't hear much of these nowadays apart from *Lakmé* and, to a lesser degree, *Le Roi l'a dit*.

Having laboured in the vineyard for many years, Delibes was rewarded with some official honours. He was made a Chevalier of the Légion d'Honour and, in 1881, became the unlikely professor of advanced composition at the Conservatoire. This appointment came through the good offices of the composer Ambroise Thomas, to whom Delibes disclaimed any knowledge of fugue or counterpoint (a bit like appointing a surgeon who hadn't studied anatomy!).

Delibes would never be on a list of the all-time great composers, but he is a worthy middlebrow, for his music is melodic and is universally known and loved.

Delibes – A Middlebrow Mix

Coppélia

Delibes was the first composer to realise that ballet music could be more than just a sequence of pretty but unconnected tunes. He felt it could operate more like a symphony or an opera, with the music outlining the story and being part of the performance's whole emotional development. *Coppélia* and *Sylvia* went a long way towards achieving this, but it remained for Tchaikovsky to take up where Delibes left off and bring the ideas of symphonic unity and a satisfying overall structure to full fruition.

The ballet *Coppélia*, subtitled 'The Girl with the Enamel Eyes' took its bow at the Paris Opéra in 1870 and was an immediate success with both audiences and critics. With its charming setting of life in an Austrian village, it was the first ballet that used as its subject the story of a doll that comes to life. With Swanhilda's csárdás it also set the fashion of incorporating folk dances into ballet music. There's a marvellous mazurka and other great tunes in *Coppélia*, which are often heard as a concert suite – it's not to be missed!

Sylvia

Sylvia was first presented at the Paris Opéra six years after *Coppélia*, and was another great success. Its subtitle is 'The Nymph of Diana', and it's a grand mythological ballet. Some characters are mortal, some are deities and others seem to have a foot in each camp. Again, there is a string of great numbers and a concert suite. The Pizzicato is especially celebrated, as is the Bacchanale, the exciting music associated with Bacchus, the god of wine and revelry.

Lakmé

This is the only opera by Delibes still in the repertoire and its survival is due largely to the opportunities given to a coloratura soprano. The title rôle attracted the finest sopranos of the time, such as Adelina Patti and Luisa Tettrazini. One of the great exponents of our time has been Joan Sutherland. *Lakmé* is set in India in the 19th century and the plot centres on the fanatical hatred of the Brahmin priests for the English invaders who forbid them to practise their religion. Gerald, a British officer, falls in love with Lakmé, the daughter of a Brahmin priest. It's a tragic tale and ends with Lakmé poisoning herself when she realises that Gerald's sense of duty will prevail over his personal feelings.

The celebrated 'Bell song' (a version of an old Brahmin song) is one of the highlights, one of those great showpieces beloved of star sopranos and their audiences – full of trills, runs and twiddly bits. Even better known nowadays is the 'Flower duet' sung by Lakmé and her servant as they glide in a small boat to a pool where the blue lotus flowers. The tune has become familiar to anyone who watches television because it was adopted by British Airways for its worldwide commercials.

GEORGES BIZET
(1838-1875)

Georges Bizet was an unfortunate character, nothing ever seemed to go right for him. He wanted nothing more than to make his name as a composer of operas, but he died at the age of 37 with his ambition unrealised. He was not to know that Tchaikovsky's prophecy would be fulfilled:

> *"I am convinced," the Russian said, "that in about ten years Carmen will have become the most popular opera in the world."*

Bizet was born in Paris and got his early training from his musical parents before being admitted to the Conservatoire at the age of nine. One of his teachers said that he possessed little trace of talent, but nevertheless the young Georges became a brilliant pianist and at the age of seventeen composed his 'Symphony in C', which is well worthy of your attention.

As a result of winning the coveted Prix de Rome, Bizet spent three years in the Italian capital. This was a happy period of his life but not very fruitful in terms of compositions. Back in Paris, things became tough. His mother had died as he was on his way home, and he had to undertake all sorts of musical chores in order to earn a living. His opera *The Pearl Fishers* wasn't much of a success, despite being praised by Berlioz and having what has become the most popular duet in all opera ('Au fond du temple saint', for tenor and baritone). *The Fair Maid of Perth* fared no better – four years later it was well reviewed but received only eighteen performances.

Bizet married the daughter of his former professor Halévy in 1869. Geneviève was a beautiful but neurotic woman and her mother suffered from bouts of insanity. Bizet's responsibilities towards them and his duties as a member of the National Guard during the Franco-Prussian war took a toll on his energy and creativity. During that period of five years or so he composed very little of note.

When Bizet finally did come up with a masterpiece, he didn't live to see it acknowledged. He is said to have left the première of *Carmen* before the end, practically in tears because

of the unresponsiveness of the audience. The critics condemned
the plot as too immoral, and found the score overlong and "scientific", although certain individual items were praised. Bizet
went into a depression, and shortly afterwards fell ill with an
attack of quinsy. This was complicated by rheumatism and an ear
infection. Two heart attacks took him out of his misery on the day
of the 23rd performance of *Carmen*, the opera that was soon to
conquer the world.

Bizet – A Middlebrow Mix

Carmen

Bizet's operatic masterpiece must take pride of place. It was
premièred in Paris in 1875, but poor old Bizet had a terrible time
on the first night. The first act was fairly well received, but each
successive act brought less applause. The composer remarked:

> *I sense defeat, I foresee a definite and hopeless flop.*

Well! His fears were well founded, but only in the short term.
After his untimely death, *Carmen* went on to become one of the
most popular operas of all time.

A sergeant of the guard, Don José, falls for a flirtatious gypsy
girl, Carmen, who works in a cigarette factory, becoming so
besotted with her that he abandons his sweetheart Micaëla, the
approved choice of his mother. Carmen is imprisoned for
wounding a fellow worker but exercises her wiles on Don José
who helps her to escape. José, in turn, is imprisoned and on his
own release joins Carmen and her gypsy friends. However, in a
fit of jealous rage José attacks his superior officer Zuniga and
has no choice but to desert his regiment and throw in his lot
with the gypsies. The fickle Carmen soon tires of him and takes
up with a bullfighter Escamillo, promising herself to him if he is
successful in the forthcoming bullfight. Carmen arrives in great
splendour at the bullring with Escamillo but when he enters the
arena she is confronted by José, who implores her to leave with
him. She says she no longer loves him and would rather die
than give up her freedom. José draws his knife and stabs her
just as Escamillo emerges triumphant. José confesses his crime
and throws himself on the body of his beloved Carmen.

Carmen is just one highlight after another, including: 'Habanera'; 'L'amour est un oiseau rebelle' (Carmen, soprano); 'Seguidilla' ; 'Près des ramparts de Séville (Carmen); 'The toreador's song (Escamillo); the flower song, 'La fleur que tu m'avais jetée' (Don José).

The *Carmen Suite* is also a must – all the great tunes brilliantly orchestrated, starting with the famous prelude. Another piece you should check out is the *Carmen Suite* for violin and orchestra by Pablo de Sarasate, a terrific showpiece for virtoso violinist with exciting variations on all the hit numbers.

The L'Arlésienne Suite

In 1872 Bizet was commissioned to provide some incidental music for the play *L'Arlésienne* ('The Girl from Arles') by Alphonse Daudet. The première in Paris was not a great success for either composer or playwright. Bizet's music was not even noticed, the public reacting with throat-clearing, coughing and lively chatter while the small orchestra was playing so that Bizet complained to Daudet, "They haven't listened once yet." The music fared better than the play, however, because Bizet quickly extracted from the score and arranged for full orchestra a suite of four numbers which was an instant hit. A second suite of four more numbers (one of which, the minuet, is actually from Bizet's opera *The Fair Maid of Perth*) was compiled after the composer's death by his friend and colleague Ernest Guiraud.

The movements of the first suite are the Prelude, Minuet, Adagietto and Carillon. The Prelude is mainly a set of variations on *The March of the Kings*, a Provençal song dating from the 18th century, while the *Carillon*, as the name implies, evokes the chiming of church bells.

'Suite No. 2' consists of a Pastorale, Intermezzo, Minuet and the hugely popular Farandole, in which *The March of the Kings* is combined with a Provençal folk tune.

Jeux d'Enfants ('Children's Games')

This consists of twelve pieces originally written for piano duet and living up to its title – lightweight and playful. Five of the pieces were orchestrated under the title *Petite Suite*. One of them, 'Le Bal', has special significance for me, it was the theme tune of a television programme I introduced back in the sixties called

Melody Fair. I sat bow-tied in a sort of opera box introducing pieces played by the RTÉ Concert Orchestra. We had a guest each weekand one was the violinist Geraldine O'Grady. That was our first meeting and it wasn't long before we were married. (We still are.)

Au Fond du Temple Saint ('In the Depths of the Temple')

This must be the most requested and most popular of all operatic duets. It comes from Bizet's final opera *The Pearl Fishers*. On a wild beach in Ceylon two pearl fishers, Zurga (baritone) and Nadir (tenor), recall how they had seen and fallen in love with a beautiful young priestess. The duet has been recorded by practically every tenor-baritone duo, but outstanding is the interpretation of Swedish tenor Jussi Björling and the American baritone Robert Merrill.

Serenade from *The Fair Maid of Perth*

This lovely tenor aria is about all we hear nowadays of the opera based on a Sir Walter Scott novel. I can particularly recommend the wonderful and celebrated interpretation by the late English tenor Heddle Nash and the more recent version by our own Frank Patterson.

Symphony No. 1 in C

Bizet was only seventeen when he composed this sparkling, vivacious work with catchy tunes throughout. It remains a mystery why no-one saw fit to perform it until 1935.

PETER TCHAIKOVSKY
(1840-1893)

Some of the intellectuals are inclined to denigrate Tchaikovsky as being too emotional, but if you're a middlebrow like me you won't complain. What's wrong with letting the emotions run riot? Tears of joy or sadness never did anyone any harm, though in Tchaikovsky's case the emotion often sank deep into anguish and despair. He was an arch Romantic with a genius for melody. He also had a flair for the dramatic but, with the exception of *Eugen Onegin*, did not seem able to translate this flair into the successful composition of operas.

Peter Ilyitch was the son of a government mine inspector. He studied law and then worked as a clerk in the ministry of justice but while clerking he enrolled at the St Petersburg Conservatory where his teacher was Anton Rubinstein, whose brother Nicholas caused Tchaikovsky much chagrin later when he bad-mouthed his 'Piano Concerto No. 1'. At the age of 23 Tchaikovsky decided to dedicate himself solely to music. Within ten years he was established at home and was the first Russian composer to win a large following abroad.

It is now accepted that Tchaikovsky was a homosexual – something with which he struggled his whole life and which caused him many bouts of severe melancholy and depression. Nevertheless, he did marry when he was 34. A young student, Antonia Milukova fancied herself in love with him and badgered him into marrying her. It became almost immediately apparent that the marriage was a disaster and Tchaikovsky suffered a severe nervous breakdown.

There were three other women in Tchaikovsky's life. The first was his mother, to whom he was almost excessively attached. She died when he was fourteen and he probably never fully recovered from the emotional trauma. When he was 28 Tchaikovsky developed a crush on a Belgian opera singer called Désirée Artôt. She ran off with a baritone and the story is that Tchaikovsky poured out his anguish in the song 'None But The Lonely Heart'.

Then, later, a very important woman entered his life. She was the 'beloved friend' Nadezhda von Meck, who supported and corresponded with him for years on condition that they should never meet. It seems that they did once pass in the street,

look at each other in embarrassment and walk hurriedly on. Tchaikovsky also spent some time at her country estate, but always during her absence. This patronage allowed the composer to write without having to keep one eye on the mighty rouble, and he was devastated when it finally came to an end.

In addition to teaching at the Moscow Conservatory, Tchaikovsky conducted in Russia and around Europe. In 1891 he visited New York to conduct a concert of his own works at the opening of Carnegie Hall. He did not enjoy the visit, though. He was lonely and homesick and went back to his homeland in a state of despondency. It was in this mood that he composed the 'Sixth Symphony' ('The Pathétique') into which he seems to have poured all that was darkest in his heart. A few days after the first performance he drank unboiled water at the height of a cholera epidemic. His reckless disregard of the consequences must lead us to the conviction that he had decided to endure no further torment in this world.

Tchaikovsky – A Middlebrow Mix

Piano Concerto No. 1 in E Minor

A black day for Tchaikovsky was the day he played his first piano concerto for the eminent musician Nicholas Rubinstein. We have an account of it from Tchaikovsky himself:

> *I played the first movement – not a single word, not even a comment. If you could only know how intolerably foolish one feels when one sets before a friend a dish of one's own making and the friend eats it and says nothing...I kept my patience and played the piece through. Silence again. "Well?," I said and I rose from the piano. Then there came gushing from Rubinstein's mouth a veritable torrent of words. It appeared that my concerto was utterly worthless – absolutely unplayable. Passages were so common-place and awkward that they could not be improved. The piece as a whole was bad, trivial, vulgar. Rubinstein pointed out many passages that needed thorough revisions and added that he would play the concerto in public if these changes were ready at a certain time. "I shall not change a single note," I answered, "and I will publish the concerto exactly as it is now."*

Tchaikovsky promptly scratched Rubinstein's name from the dedication page and substitued that of Hans von Bülow, an established German pianist and conductor who took the composition to America and gave it its first performance in Boston the following year.

Eventually both Tchaikovsky and Rubinstein yielded some ground. The composer did make certain revisions and the pianist did perform the piece in Russia and Paris. To be fully effective the Tchaikovsky concerto needs a pianist of great virtuosity. I have heard it a number of times in the concert hall but the most exciting performance I ever heard was recently in the National Concert Hall in Dublin when the soloist with our National Symphony Orchestra was the brilliant Russian Grigori Sokolov. The opening is immediately arresting with French horns and orchestra giving the piano a majestic introduction and the melody then alternating between piano and orchestra. The second movement is a gentle lullaby with a little scherzo-like interlude and finally we have a boisterous dance tune, peasant-like and very Russian, bringing the concerto to a vigorous conclusion.

Violin Concerto in D

Tchaikovsky started work on his violin concerto shortly after his disastrous marriage to Antonia Milukova in 1877. He learned that his newfound benefactress Nadezhda von Meck was willing to provide him with a generous annuity and this enabled him for the first time to give up teaching, on which he had depended for his existence, and to devote his time entirely to composition. He was helped in the composition of his violin concerto by Yosif Kottek, an accomplished violinist and former composition student of his. However, when the concerto was finished, Tchaikovsky decided to dedicate it to the well-known virtuoso Leopold Auer, who promptly spurned the piece because he considered it to be unplayable.

The concerto lay rejected for a few years until Adolf Brodsky took it up and gave it its first performance in Vienna. It was not an immediate success: in fact one critic, Eduard Hanslick, wrote:

> *Tchaikovsky's violin concerto leads us for the first time to the horrible idea that there may be music that stinks in the ear.*

Brodsky, however, continued to champion the concerto and was responsible for its Moscow and London premières. In gratitude Tchaikovsky rededicated the work to him. Auer also relented and became one of the concerto's finest exponents and introduced it to his pupils, who included Mischa Elman and Jascha Heifetz. I doubt if either of those two gentlemen would have had difficulty with it.

The first movement is lyrical throughout, with moments of great excitement. Then follows a movement which Tchaikovsky aptly called 'canzonetta', a little song. This is so delicate that he doesn't even finish it, but leaps into a dazzling rondo finale.

Symphony No. 6 ('Pathétique')

The title 'Pathétique' was suggested to the composer by his brother Modest, after the score's completion in 1893. Modest also wrote an explanation of the symphony, with an assurance that it took account of thoughts which the composer had expressed in conversation.

The fourth movement, the great adagio, represented Tchaikovsky's spiritual state during the last years of his life: the bitter disappointment and profound sorrow of having to recognise that even his artistic fame was transient and incapable of alleviating his dread of eternal nothingness. The symphony is not all gloom and doom, however: the second movement is airy and graceful and the third is a mighty march.

Tchaikovsky himself conducted the first performance in St Petersburg in 1893. One week later he was dead.

1812 Overture

The '1812 Overture' is more often heard out of doors than in concert halls, probably because the cannons are less liable to do damage there. Tchaikovsky composed the piece in 1880 at the suggestion of his publisher and it was heard for the first time in the great Kremlin Square in Moscow in 1882. The occasion was the celebration of the Russian victory in 1812 that checked Napoleon's invasion. Tchaikovsky used the Russian and French national anthems as his main themes, and the piece builds up to a jubilant climax as the hymn 'God Preserve Thy People' rings out in final victory. Tchaikovsky was a bit self-conscious about the overture. He felt that it turned out too noisy and sensational to do him much credit, but it does have charm as well as bombast and perhaps the composer was overly dismissive of it as being "of purely local and patriotic significance" .

Fantasy Overture: Romeo and Juliet

There was a romantic notion that Tchaikovsky's fantasy overture 'Romeo and Juliet' was inspired by the composer's infatuation with the Belgian opera singer Désirée Artôt. The time was December 1868 and during that month the 28-year-old composer was radiantly happy. However, his state of euphoria was brief because soon after their first parting in 1869, the alluring Mme Artôt returned from Warsaw where, without warning, she had married the popular baritone Mariano Padilla.

To this unhappy experience can be attributed some of the rhapsodic elements of the 'Romeo and Juliet' music, but it does now seem clear that Tchaikovsky was not too put out by the whole business. The truth was that the 'Romeo and Juliet' theme was suggested to Tchaikovsky by Diaghilev, who recognised the budding genius of the inexperienced and as yet unknown composer. The piece has a tremendous emotional intensity, and we all know the exquisite love music which dominates the overture. There is also the thrilling depiction of the confrontation between Montagues and Capulets.

Capriccio Italien

In February 1880, while on a holiday in Rome, Tchaikovsky wrote to his benefactress Madame von Meck that he had attached a rough draft of an Italian fantasia based on popular tunes. He told her he thought it had a bright future and would be effective because of the wonderful melodies he had happened to pick up, partly from publishers' collections and partly from some he had heard in the streets. He was right: the 'Capriccio Italien' did prove to be an immediate and lasting success.

Serenade for Strings

Tchaikovsky himself loved this piece. In fact, just after composing it in 1880 he wrote to his publisher:

> *I don't know whether it is because it is my latest offspring or because it really isn't bad, but I am terribly in love with this serenade.*

He was also gratified that it was well received by his former mentor Anton Rubinstein (the one who had savaged his piano concerto). Tchaikovsky wrote the serenade at the same time as the *1812 Overture*, which he felt had no artistic value – a case of chalk and cheese? The second movement is the Viennese-like waltz which is universally known and loved.

Eugen Onegin

Tchaikovsky once wrote:

> *To refrain from writing operas is the act of a hero and we have only one such hero in our time – Brahms. Such heroism is not for me. The stage, with all its glitter, attracts me irresistibly.*

He was replying to the suggestion of his benefactress Madame von Meck that his gifts might be more profitably applied to purely instrumental music.

Of the ten operas he wrote, Tchaikovsky had only one lasting success. This is *Eugen Onegin*, which was based on a poem by the Russian epic poet Alexander Pushkin. He wrote it around the time that he was having the disastrous episode with Antonia Milukova – the student who he should never have married. Initial productions were modest and the reactions reserved, but when the Imperial Opera produced it in St Petersburg in 1882 it suddenly began to enjoy the success that made it a rival in popularity to Glinka's *A Life for the Tsar*. The opera itself is not high on the list of middlebrow favourites but the orchestral dances are musts – particularly the waltz and the polonaise.

Swan Lake

Tchaikovsky composed his ballet *Swan Lake* on a commission from the Bolshoi Theatre in 1877. He said he undertook it because he needed the money and also because he had long entertained the wish to try his hand at this sort of music, having admired the work of Delibes for many years. He was not content to write a classical ballet in the conventional style but created an entirely new kind of dramatic ballet score, using in the process some pieces he had previously composed for voice and piano.

The first production was a failure due mainly to poor performance and choreography. The honour of creating the role of Odette-Odile fell to a mediocre ballerina who had one powerful advantage over her colleagues – an influential husband who was a Greek industrialist. The choreographer was a German called Reisinger, one report said that:

> *If Reisinger did not display the artistry that should go with his calling, he showed a remarkable skill in arranging a sort of gymnastic exercises instead of dances. The* corps de ballet *stamp in one and the same spot, waving their hands like the sails of windmills, while the soloists jump around the stage with gymnastic steps.*

The ballet was never again performed in Tchaikovsky's lifetime and it was twenty years before *Swan Lake*, with an entirely new production and new choreography by Marius Petipa, became an acknowledged masterpiece.

I don't know if you know the story of the ballet but, very briefly, it concerns the princess Odette who has been bewitched by her evil stepmother. By day she is a swan and at night she reverts to human form. Prince Siegfried meets the Swan Maiden, falls in love with her and promises to choose her as his bride at a ball to be held the following evening. Only in this way can the evil spell be broken. Things go wrong, however. The prince is tricked into choosing a girl who has been transformed into the likeness of Odette. Heartbroken, Odette rushes back to the lake. Siegfried follows to beg her forgiveness but in a great storm the waves rise and engulf the two lovers.

There are recordings of the entire score, but you would probably be better off getting a suite with a selection of the most popular numbers or, better still, a CD with the highlights of all three of Tchaikovsky's ballet masterpieces.

The Sleeping Beauty

When Tchaikovsky had put the finishing touches to his ballet *The Sleeping Beauty*, he wrote to Madame von Meck:

> *I think, dear friend, that this ballet will be one of my best works. The subject is so poetical, so grateful for the musical setting, that I was carried away while composing it and wrote it with such warmth and enthusiasm that my feelings must surely be reflected in the music.*

The first performance was given in St Petersburg in 1890 with choreography by the renowned Marius Petipa, but it fared little better than had *Swan Lake* thirteen years earlier. The audience was apathetic and the critics scornful. The Tsar attended the first performance and, damning with faint praise, said that it was "very nice". It was only after the composer's death that the greatness of *The Sleeping Beauty* was acknowledged. Stravinksy called it a masterpiece and praised the music's freshness, inventiveness, ingenuity and vigour.

It is based on the familiar fairytale of the princess who pricks her finger on a rose thorn and, pursuant to the curse of the wicked witch, falls into a hundred-year sleep. It doesn't, of course, last quite that long – she is woken after a while by the kiss of a prince. One of the highlights is the great Rose Adagio, then there is the celebrated waltz and lots of delightful numbers. Again a suite made up of excerpts is a very good idea.

The Nutcracker Suite

Tchaikovsky's ballet *The Nutcracker* was first performed in St Petersburg in December 1892, and like its two predecessors was not an immediate success – in spite of the introduction of the 'celesta', a little piano-like instrument with a tinkling sound. Tchaikovsky first heard this in Paris and was captivated by its "divinely wonderful" tones. He couldn't wait to introduce it to St Petersburg, but was determined to keep it under wraps so that Rimsky-Korsakov couldn't get to hear it and use it before he could.

The Nutcracker was based on a fairytale by E. T. A. Hoffman. A little girl, Marie, receives a nutcracker as a Christmas gift. Stealing downstairs during the night to see her new toy, she is overtaken by a troupe of mice. The Nutcracker and all the other toys come to life and a battle ensues. The Nutcracker is almost killed but, rescued by Marie, is transformed magically into a handsome young prince. The two of them journey together to the Kingdom of Sweets – a domain that looks like anyone's dream of Fairyland and definitely good enough to eat. It is here that the divertissement is performed from which comes four of the dances in the *Nutcracker Suite*: the 'Russian Dance', 'Arabian Dance', 'Chinese Dance' and the 'Dance of the Flutes' (or 'Mirlitons', as it's sometimes known). The other numbers in the suite are the 'Miniature Overture', 'March', 'Dance of the Sugar Plum Fairy', featuring the silvery-toned celesta, and finally the great 'Waltz of the Flowers', one of the best loved and most brilliant of Tchaikovsky's waltzes.

An unusual thing about the *Nutcracker Suite* is that it pre-ceded the première of the ballet by about nine months.

OTHER MID-ROMANTIC NOTEWORTHIES

Louis Hérold
(1791-1883)

In 1831 the French composer Hérold had a brilliant success at the Opéra Comique in Paris with *Zampa*, or *The Marble Bride*. The second title is explained by the dénouement of the plot. After a life of cruelty and plunder and womanising, the pirate Zampa comes to a sticky end when he is crushed to death by the statue of a girl he had led astray. "This is the stuff of comic opera?" I hear you ask. Well, for some reason, the French found talking within an opera terribly amusing, so anything with spoken passages – even a tragedy – is automatically called Opéra Comique. This can be quite confusing, since half the time you're not sure until it's too late whether you're supposed to laugh or cry. One way to tell, perhaps, is to look at the stage just before the curtain falls. If anyone is left standing, it was a comedy. The overture to Zampa is tuneful from beginning to end, and is one of the most requested on *Music for Middlebrows*.

Ambroise Thomas
(1811-1896)

The career of Ambroise Thomas mingled success and failure to a remarkable degree over a long period of time. He composed twenty operas in all, but was over 50 years of age when he had his first resounding success with the operas *Mignon* and *Hamlet* and, though he lived another 30 years or so, he never managed to repeat these triumphs. But he did experience the rare thrill of seeing *Mignon* receive its 1,000th performance – a gala occasion at the Opéra Comique in 1894, just two years before his death, for which he received the Grand Cross of the Legion d'Honneur.

The overture to *Mignon* abounds in good tunes, most of which come straight from the opera itself. Some of his juniors, however, did not think much of the music and weren't shy about saying so even though he was director of the Paris Conservatoire, a position he held for a quarter of a century. But it's a massively enjoyable piece and their opinions needn't concern us.

He followed *Mignon* in 1868 with a treatment of *Hamlet* in five acts, something that was considered worthy of production at the Paris Opéra itself. It proved to be a success, and did a lot for the prestige of M. Thomas. The opera, according to custom, had to have a ballet and it is in this delightful music that many of its charms can be found.

Friedrich von Flotow
(1812-1883)

The German composer Flotow was born a nobleman and educated for the diplomatic service, but he discovered in himself a gift for music and devoted himself to writing for the theatre. Of his twenty-odd operas, the one for which he is chiefly remembered is *Martha*, which was first heard in Vienna in 1847.

The setting is England during the reign of Queen Anne (early 18th century). Lady Harriet, maid of honour to the Queen, is bored with court life and disguises herself as a working girl (Martha). She and her maid get jobs on a farm but find the going too tough. However, the young farmers fall in love with them and vice versa and – surprise, surprise! – one of them (Lyonel) turns out to be a nobleman, so all ends happily. The two hit numbers are 'Ach so fromm' (better known in its Italian version 'M'appari') sung by the lovesick Lyonel and 'The last rose of summer', Moore's melody borrowed unashamedly by Flotow for the eponymous Martha.

Henry Litolff
(1818-1891)

Litolff was born in London but was of Alsatian descent. He first achieved fame as a travelling piano virtuoso, and then became a successful music publisher. He composed a number of pieces for himself to play, including the five 'Concertos Symphoniques'. He must have felt that these works for piano and orchestra were a cut above being simple concertos, and they certainly are symphonic in scale, with infectious tunes and novel interplay between solo instrument and orchestra. The scherzo from 'Symphony-Concerto No. 4' is one of the most sparkling pieces in the entire repertoire, with the soloist dancing deftly over the keyboard. It's known simply as the 'Litolff Scherzo' and is a must if ever there was one.

Franz von Suppé
(1819-1895)

Franz von Suppé was born in Smit, Dalmatia, of a Belgian father
and an Austrian mother. He was largely Italianised, his family
having lived at Cremona for three generations and was merci-
fully always known by his abbreviated name as the full thing
was (wait for it) Francesco Ezechiele Ermenegildo Cavaliere Suppé
-Demelli. In spite of his early interest in music, Suppé was intended for the legal profession and was able to pursue his real
vocation only when, on the death of his father in 1835, he moved
with his mother to her native Vienna. Not long afterwards he
secured a small post as theatre conductor. More important posts
of the same sort followed, and for the last 30 years of his life he
was in charge of music at the historic Theater an der Wien.

Suppé's output of operettas in the 19th century made
everybody else look like layabouts. He wrote the music for about
150 stage works and is credited with having created the Viennese
operetta. He got the idea from Jacques Offenbach, who visited
Vienna in 1858, and he paved the way for Strauss, Millöcker,
Lehár and others. Oddly enough, Suppé was proclaimed the
German Offenbach, though the real Offenbach was a native of
Cologne.

The operettas of Franz von Suppé have had an almost
exclusively Viennese popularity but many of the overtures are
popular the world over. It would be a close call between the
Light Cavalry and *Poet and Peasant* as to which is the most popular.
Both are in the repertoire of any self-respecting band or light
orchestra. *Light Cavalry* was first produced in 1866 and poked
cheerful fun at the idea of military glamour unaccompanied by
corresponding military prowess. The overture, from the opening
trumpet call to the brilliant conclusion, leaves little doubt in one's
mind as to the subject matter of the work.

César Franck
(1822-1890)

It was said of the Belgian composer César Franck that "he seemed
to be surrounded by music as by a halo". He was a modest little
man with bushy side whiskers and ill-fitting clothes. If you

happened upon him walking in the streets of Paris, talking and gesticulating to himself – something which was often quite startling to passers-by – he would be the last person you would imagine at the heart of a vehement musical controversy. Franck was far more generously disposed towards his contemporaries than most of them were towards him: he received only the minimum of recognition during his lifetime.

Franck was known for his marvellous improvisations at the organ, which held listeners spellbound. He was 50 when he became professor at the Paris Conservatoire, and it was as 'Professor of Organ' rather than as composer that he was finally awarded the ribbon of the Légion d'Honneur. Franck was kept so busy teaching and playing that he got up at five o'clock every morning to give himself some time to compose.

He was held in admiration and affection by his students, and had it not been for their efforts, he might well have remained unknown as a composer. But with the help of the National Society of Music, they organised a Franck Festival in 1887 which at least brought his works to the attention of the public. But at least one fellow composer thought well of him: Debussy is recorded as saying that:

> *He was a man without guile. The discovery of a beautiful harmony was enough to make him happy. He possessed the soul of a child and, though he was unfortunate and unrecognised, nothing could make him feel bitter.*

It was not until the age of 67 that his only symphony, on which he had worked for years, was grudgingly performed by the Conservatoire Orchestra. The musicians were uninterested and the audience perplexed and the experts raised their hands in horror. Franck was certainly a creator in advance of his time and it was only in the last year of his life that he could say that the public was beginning to understand him. The 'Symphony in D Minor', however, is a mighty work, and gradually it worked its way into the hearts of millions, becoming one of the most popular and performed symphonies of all.

His 'Sonata for Violin and Piano in A Major' was composed in 1886 as a wedding present for the famous Belgian violinist and composer Eugene Ysaÿe. It's not in traditional sonata form, as the principal movement comes second, the first being a graceful and quiet preamble. The work has a melodic charm second to none, with themes recurring in all four movements. It's easy to understand the instant and enduring success of this sonata, it's one of the most popular for violin and piano and, if you feel like cutting your teeth on sonatas, look no further.

One of the few occasions when an audience greeted Franck's music with any warmth was in 1882. He was conducting an early mass of his, and at the last minute had added the 'Panis Angelicus'. This was considered the most beautiful part of the work. It was received enthusiastically, even encored, and has remained enormously popular ever since. There is a famous recording by John McCormack with the lovely violin obbligato played by his friend Fritz Kreisler.

Édouard Lalo
(1823-1892)

Lalo was one of the many French composers who were fascinated by the culture and music of Spain, though in Lalo's case it was not surprising as he was of Spanish descent. He was one of the most distinguished French composers of his time and deserving of the Légion d'Honneur conferred on him in 1890. Not many of his works are performed these days, with the exception of the great 'Symphonie Espagnole' for solo violin and orchestra. This dates from 1873 and was first played by the Spanish virtuoso Pablo de Sarasate, for whom it was written. About the title, the composer said:

> *I kept the title,* Symphonie Espagnole, *contrary to and despite everybody, first because it conveyed my thought, that is to say, a violin solo soaring above the rigid form of an old symphony and then again because the title was less banal than those which were proposed to me.*

For some reason, Lalo did not seem to want people to think of this work as a concerto. As well as calling it a symphony, he also gave it five movements, though the third is often left out in concert performance. The Spanish element is evident throughout the work, especially in the rhythm, and there is a wealth of melody to delight the ear.

The opening allegro is the most symphonic and it is followed by a little scherzo based on a rhythm known as a seguidilla. Then follows the intermezzo, more often heard on recordings than in the concert hall. It's actually a slower scherzo dominated by the soloist. The fourth movement is more turbulent than tranquil and then the rondo finale provides the work with a typical symphonic finale.

Alexander Borodin
(1833-1887)

The composition which contributed more than anything to the international fame of Alexander Borodin was the musical picture *In the Steppes of Central Asia*. This was dedicated to Franz Liszt, who had introduced Borodin's music to western Europe. *In the Steppes of Central Asia* is based on a programme which the composer outlined as follows:

> *In the monotonous sandy wastes of the Central Asian Steppes there arises the hitherto unfamiliar sound of a peaceful Russian song. From the distance can be heard the tramping of horses and camels and a strange Oriental melody. An Asiatic caravan approaches. Under the protection of Russian weapons, it makes its way safely and untroubled across the measureless waste. It passes, then gradually moves off into the distance. The song of the Russians and the Asiatic melody are combined in a common harmony, whose echoes are gradually lost in the air of the Steppes.*

Borodin was in fact a distinguished professor of chemistry who did a little composing on the side. He once wrote:

> *I can only compose when I am too unwell to give lectures. So my friends, reversing the usual custom, never say to me, "I hope you are well" but rather "I do hope you are ill".*

His musical work was constantly subordinated to his scientific activities, which accounts for his small output as a composer and the fact that he never actually finished *Prince Igor*, though he worked at it on and off for the last eighteen years of his life. The opera was completed and orchestrated after his death by Rimsky-Korsakov and Glazunov. Rimsky-Korsakov was in fact always interested in Borodin's music and often embarrassed his friend with pressing offers of advice and assistance.

Prince Igor is best known to us through the 'Polovtsian Dances'. The Polovtsi were a race of Tartars who held sway in 12th century Central Asia. They capture Prince Igor and his son Vladimir but treat them rather well. In fact, the Tartar leader Khan Konchak puts on an entertainment in their honour, the highlight of which is a series of tribal dances. Borodin wrote wonderful music for these dances – at times hauntingly beautiful and at other times wild and exciting. The sequence builds up to a breathtaking grand finale with the entrance of the warriors. You may remember the musical *Kismet* some years ago, which borrowed the music of Borodin for all its hit numbers: 'Stranger In Paradise', 'This Is My Beloved' etc.

Another Borodin must is the wonderful melody from 'String Quartet No. 2', known in orchestral form as 'Nocturne'.

Amilcare Ponchielli
(1834-1886)

The fame of the Italian composer Ponchielli rests solely on his opera *La Gioconda*. It was first performed at La Scala, Milan, in 1876, and was hailed by the critics as worthy of ranking with Verdi. It was loosely based on a play by Victor Hugo and, along with Verdi's *Aida*, which preceded it by a few years, it represents the spectacular and grandiose style which shows the influence of French grand opera and people like Meyerbeer.

It seems that Ponchielli was afflicted by torturing self-doubt and arrived at his ideas by a painful process of trial and error. However, the ballet sequence 'The Dance of the Hours' was composed at a single sitting and turned out to be the most memorable part of the work. The tunes are known to all, one being used by American comedian Alan Sherman for his hit 'Hello mudda, hello fadda' some years ago, and the galop brings the divertissement to an exhilarating conclusion.

Henryk Wieniawski
(1835-1880)

Polish violinist Henryk Wieniawski entered the Paris Conservatoire at the age of eight and quickly made an international name as a brilliant soloist. For eleven years he was court violinist in St Petersburg, and he spent the rest of his short life (he was only 44 when he died) travelling in Europe and North America.

He suffered from a heart ailment which caused him a lot of problems. On one occasion he started to play his second concerto in Berlin but was unable to continue. The great Joseph Joachim, who happened to be in the audience, stepped onto the platform, took up Wieniawski's violin and said, "Although I cannot play my dear friend's wonderful concerto, I shall play Bach's *Chaconne*." This gesture was much appreciated.

Wieniawski did a tour of the USA with the Russian pianist Anton Rubinstein, but for most of the time they were not on speaking terms due to the fact that Rubinstein's name sometimes appeared in larger print on the posters. Artistes can still be very sensitive about that sort of thing!

Of Wieniawski's shorter compositions, the most popular is the lovely 'Légende', which is full of tenderness and lyricism. This was composed under the spell of his love for an Englishwoman, Isobel Hampton. She must have been impressed because she became his wife. Other popular ones of the showpiece variety are 'Polacca Brillante' and 'Scherzo-Tarantelle'.

The masterpiece, though, is 'Concerto No. 2 in D Minor', first performed in 1862 by the composer though it was dedicated to the Spanish virtuoso Pablo de Sarasate. This was one of the most popular violin concertos in the world at one time. It is an absolute beauty, with an exquisite Romance as the second movement and an irresistible finale marked *à la zingara* – in gypsy style.

Modeste Mussorgsky
(1839-1881)

The year 1874 was an important one in the short life of Modeste Mussorgsky. After two rejections and three years of writing, rewriting and compromise, his masterpiece *Boris Godunov* was finally given its first performance in St Petersburg and turned out to be the one public triumph of his career. Later that same year Mussorgsky produced another work, *Pictures at an Exhibition*, which, with the passing of time, has become as well known as his *Boris*.

Pictures at an Exhibition was written in memory of the painter and architect Victor Hartmann and comprises ten musical pictures, interspersed with promenades representing the composer arriving at the exhibition and walking through the gallery, pausing here and there to study a picture. The best known picture is 'The Great Gate at Kiev', based on Hartmann's design for a fantastical Triumphal Arch that was never built. Originally written for piano, it is now more often heard in the magical orchestral version by Maurice Ravel. 'The Great Gate' brings the whole work to a tremendous climax – one of the most sonorous and dazzling you will ever hear.

Emmanuel Chabrier
(1841-1894)

At the age of fifteen, Emmanuel Chabrier came to Paris and entered the Civil Service. While there he associated with poets, painters and musicians, and enjoyed amongst these people the reputation of a brilliant pianist. In his mid-thirties he successfully produced a comic opera, resigned his government post and became assistant to the great conductor Lamoureux, helping him in the early Paris performances of Wagner, to whose music he was greatly devoted.

But the most significant event of his life was an extended holiday he took with his family in Spain in 1882. He was deeply impressed by the folk music he heard – the tunes and wide variety of rhythms. The Spanish señoras and señoritas also caught his attention and he made reference to the fact that they often had trouble remembering to do up their bathing costumes. All these impressions gave rise to the famous *España*. This is based on tunes he heard in Spain and is a breezy, evocative Spanish piece, embellished with the distinctive sound of castanets. The principal theme was in the Hit Parade in the 1950s with the unlikely song title 'Hot Diggity'.

THE LATE-ROMANTICS (1880-1910)

CAMILLE SAINT-SAËNS
(1835-1921)

Camille Saint-Saëns said of himself that he produced music "as an apple tree produces apples". He was certainly one of the most gifted musicians of the 19th century – a prodigy of Mozartian proportions who went on to be hailed by no less a person than Liszt as "the world's greatest organist". He was an all-rounder too, being gifted in departments other than music. His interests included painting, philosophy, astronomy, literature and theatre, and he wrote knowledgeably about all of them.

Saint-Saëns made his first concert appearance when he was about six and by the time he reached double figures he was playing concertos by Mozart and Beethoven. He entered the Paris Conservatoire when he was thirteen and won numerous prizes there, though never the prestigious Prix de Rome. His precocious gifts won the admiration of big guns, such as Gounod and Rossini, though Berlioz once remarked that "he knows everything but lacks experience". Saint-Saëns became organist at the Madeleine, a post he held for twenty years. He was co-founder of the Societé Nationale de la Musique, which promoted new French music and encouraged young composers.

He has been called the French Mendelssohn and he certainly had great skill and wrote delightful music but is thought to have lacked fire in his belly. He produced over the years an enormous amount of music in every known form and was envied by some contemporaries for the great success he achieved with apparently little effort. One outspoken begrudger was Mussorgsky "a utiliser of miniatures, a creative crumb" was how he summed up the French master Another begrudger said later, "That's certainly bad music, but it's well written." Saint-Saëns's own big disappointment was that his operas didn't achieve the same success as most of his other compositions. Only *Samson and Delilah* made the grade, though it was first rejected by the Paris Opéra and instead was premièred by Liszt in Weimar.

Saint-Saëns lived a long time and became the eminence grise of French music. He travelled as far afield as South Africa and the USA: he actually gave an organ recital in San Francisco at the age of 80. That wouldn't be so remarkable in today's jet age, but it was something else in 1915. But he did suffer tragedy in his life, losing two children within weeks, and was not always the most courteous and even-tempered of men. He was 86 when he died in Algeria and he has been summed up as "organist, pianist, caricaturist, dabbler in science, enamoured of mathematics and astronomy, amateur comedian, critic, traveller, archaeologist – he was a restless man" . He was also a friend of the notorious Mata Hari, the Dutch *femme fatale* shot by the French as a spy. How did he find time to write all that music?

Saint-Saëns – A Middlebrow Mix

Carnival of the Animals

Carnival of the Animals is probably the most popular of all the compositions of Saint-Saëns. He called it "a grand zoological fantasy" and he must have been afraid that it would affect his reputation as a serious composer, because he forbade its public performance soon after its introduction at a privately held concert. The only number that escaped the embargo was 'The Swan', which became a favourite salon piece and is still the most popular cello solo in the world.

Scored for two pianos and orchestra (originally for a small orchestral ensemble), the *Carnival of the Animals* pokes fun at Offenbach, Berlioz, Mendelssohn, Rossini and indeed Saint-Saëns himself. The tortoises dance Offenbach's famous 'Can-can' at the slowest possible speed; the elephant cavorts to the 'Dance of the Slyphs' from Berlioz's *The Damnation of Faust* and also trips the light fantastic to the strains of Mendelssohn's scherzo from *A Midsummer Night's Dream*.

In 'Fossils', the xylophone is featured, with Saint-Saëns giving us, among other tunes, his own *Dance Macabre*, and this has a very effective recap in the finale. Other animals included in the menagerie are the lion, the kangaroos and the "personages with long ears" – could these be the critics? Perish the thought! The two solo pianists are called upon to send themselves up with their maddeningly hesitant scales and arpeggios.

Carnival of the Animals is now often performed with the brilliant verses of Ogden Nash, which conclude with the memorable couplet:

In outdoing Barnum and Bailey and Ringling
Saint-Saëns has done a miraculous thingling.

Samson and Delilah

This was the only great operatic success for Saint-Saëns. The
Paris public loved it and it became wildly popular. The plot, of
course, is the well-known one about Delilah tempting Samson
to reveal the fact that his strength is in his hair. The big aria is
'Mon coeur s'ouvre à ta voix ('Softly awakes my heart'), one of
the most popular of all mezzo arias. Also very popular with middlebrows is the ballet music – particularly the exciting Bacchanale.

Violin Music

Saint-Saëns wrote wonderfully for the violin. One of my personal favourites is 'Violin Concerto No. 3', which has such lovely
melody throughout. Then there are the two great pieces for solo
violin and orchestra – Introduction and Rondo Capriccioso, a
brilliant showpiece and the 'Havanaise', a gentle, melodic piece
based on a Spanish dance.

Danse Macabre

This is the most popular of the four tone poems which were influenced by those of Franz Liszt. Death, in the guise of an off-
key fiddler, sits on a tombstone and tries to tune his violin. The
sound conjures up the skeletons from the graves and they dance
about, bones rattling, getting wilder and wilder until the cock
crows at dawn and they retire back to the earth. The favourite
instrument for skeletons is, of course, the xylophone. (Sir Thomas
Beecham once said that the instrument sounded to him like skeletons copulating on a tin roof!)

Symphony No. 3 ('Organ' Symphony)

This work was written " to the memory of Franz Liszt" but
there is nothing funereal about it. You will detect a little 'Dies
Irae' quote but Saint-Saëns doesn't dwell on it. In fact as soon as
we begin to say "that sounds familiar", he changes the tune and
goes off in another direction. I will never again be able to hear
this symphony without thinking of the film *Babe* and that
incredible dance (Lughnasa eat your heart out) performed by

the farmer when he realises that his pet pig is recovering. The finale of the symphony is one of the greatest sounds you will ever hear and was appropriately chosen to inaugurate the new organ at the National Concert Hall in Dublin, with Gerard Gillen doing the honours.

ANTONIN DVORAK
(1841-1904)

Antonin Dvorak's father was a butcher and an innkeeper in a little Bohemian village, but he also liked music and song. He played the fiddle a bit and tinkled zither accompaniments while his customers danced on the village green. It was presumed that Antonin would follow in his father's footsteps, but the music appealed to him much more. As a boy he picked up the folksongs and dances with ease, played them on the fiddle and absorbed them into his being. He was later able to tap this rich source as a composer.

It wasn't long before father Dvorak realised that his son wasn't cut out to be a butcher. He allowed him to go off to the organ school in Prague. After studying and almost starving for a few years, Dvorak got a job playing viola in the orchestra of the Czech National Theatre. Here he came under the influence of Smetana, who was conductor of the orchestra, and who had returned to Prague from Sweden aflame with the ambition of creating a national school of music.

About ten years later Dvorak obtained a good position as church organist. He was able to give up orchestral playing and devote more time to composition. He also married a professional singer, and they had nine children – although the first three died in infancy.

During his twenties Dvorak caught a dose of Wagneritis – a couple of early attempts at opera were in fact nothing more than bad Wagner. However, he soon grew out of this and found his true *métier*. He was given a small pension on the strength of his Moravian (vocal) duets, after which came the 'Slavonic Dances' which caught everybody's attention and launched him internationally.

Dvorak travelled a great deal. Like Mendelssohn, he was a great favourite in Britain, which he visited on nine separate occasions. He spent three years in America (see 'New World Symphony'), after which he became director of the Prague Conservatory. He was much honoured in later life, picking up honorary degrees and gold medals but he was happiest in the company of his pidgeons on his estate in Southern Bohemia. It was his passion for railways that led to his unexpected death.

Early in April 1904, an orgy of engine-spotting in cold weather
brought on a bad chill. Complications ensued and he died a few
weeks later.

  Dvorak's music is the essence of Bohemia. While rarely using
actual folk tunes, he wrote in their fashion – Dvorak was an
industrious composer, producing nine symphonies, nine operas,
concertos for piano, cello and violin and lots of other works. His
music is always beautifully melodic. He never seemed to lose the
innocent freshness of his village childhood, and wrote easy-to-
hear music from the heart – he's a real middlebrow.

Dvorak – A Middlebrow Mix

Symphony No. 9 ('From the New World')

In 1892 Dvorak received an invitation to head the newly established National Conservatory of Music in New York. The idea of
journeying to the United States, and of braving the great stretch
of water to get there, held little appeal for the continental Dvorak.
However, the salary he was offered – a salary fabulous in terms
of his native Bohemia – helped him overcome his hesitation. He
went to America and once there he quickly adapted himself to
his own environment. He actually found a home away from home
in Spillville, Iowa, a tiny farm community of Czech immigrants
who preserved the language and culture of their homeland. In
1893 the composer spent a blissful and productive summer there
with his wife and six children.

The 'New World Symphony' is a reflection of Dvorak's impressions of and experiences in America, but he dismissed as
nonsense statements that he used Indian or American motifs in
the work. "I merely wrote," he said, "in the spirit of American
folk songs."

The music is infectious, each movement filled with melodies
and rhythms that at once remind you of American and Bohemian folk music perfectly blended together. In some way, the
symphony is more of a fond look back towards home than a
tribute to the New World itself. Particularly memorable is the
'Largo', one of the best known and loveliest of all symphonic
melodies. It is ushered in by the cor anglais and then taken up by
other instruments. I suppose it was inevitable that words would
be put to it – it's not a bad song, called 'Goin' Home'.

Slavonic Dances

It was said of Anton Dvorak that "his music was best when it
smacked of the soil and the dances dear to his own people". No
music of his could fit that description more closely that the
'Slavonic Dances'. Dvorak composed the first set in 1878 and
someone said that it was like "an injection of monkey glands
into the concert halls and drawing rooms of Europe". The dances
brought Dvorak his first taste of success at the advanced age of
37, and paved the way for the international success of other

works. Eight years later he produced another set of dances which
were equally successful.

Dvorak actually had Brahms to thank for the commission
to write the 'Slavonic Dances' in the first place. Brahms introduced the impecunious Dvorak to his own publisher, writing in
his letter of introduction:

> *I took much pleasure in the works of Dvorak of Prague.*
> *Decidedly he is a very talented man. Besides, he is poor.*
> *Please take him into consideration.*

Dvorak was duly commissioned to write some 'Slavonic Dances'
along the lines of Brahms's 'Hungarian Dances'.

He wrote them initially as four-handed piano pieces, but
they proved so popular that he was asked to orchestrate them –
it's the orchestral version that we usually hear these days.

As a child Dvorak entertained the customers at his father's
inn by playing folk tunes on the violin. He may not have directly
quoted those tunes in the 'Slavonic Dances', but his inventions
are very similar in style and rhythm. The first set is unmistak-
ably Bohemian, while the second is influenced more by Yugosla-
vian and Russian folk music.

Carnival Overture

This exhilarating piece started life as the middle of a trilogy called
'Nature, Life and Love'. To describe it I could not improve on
Dvorak's own words:

> *The lonely, contemplative wanderer reaches the city at night-*
> *fall, where a carnival of pleasure reigns supreme. On every*
> *side is heard the clangour of instruments, mingled with*
> *shouts of joy and the unrestrained hilarity of people giving*
> *vent to their feelings in their songs and dance tunes.*

Other Dvorak Must-Hears

'Serenade for Strings' has five movements with a string of
Irresistible melodies delectably scored. *Rusalka* is clearly Dvorak's
most successful and popular opera. It's a fairytale all about a
water nymph who becomes human to gain the love of a prince.
However, there are conditions and they do not live happily ever

after. The outstanding piece is 'Hymn to the moon' – a middlebrow must. For many years this glorious melody for soprano was all that was known abroad of Dvorak's large operatic output. 'Songs my Mother Taught Me' (from 'Gypsy Songs', Opus 55) is a lovely sentimental ballad that's familiar both as a song and as an instrumental piece – particularly beloved of string players. And there are a number of piano pieces with the title 'Humoresque', but the one that's best known is in G flat, from Opus No. 101, composed in 1894.

ARTHUR SULLIVAN
(1842-1900)

The name of Arthur Sullivan is inextricably linked with that of William Gilbert, his collaborator on all those marvellous operettas. However, Sullivan yearned to be recognised as a "serious" composer, and even at the height of his success and popularity, he contrived to turn out "worthy" compositions which he hoped would impress the English musical establishment.

Sullivan's father was a bandmaster, so the handsome, curly-headed Arthur played with band instruments from the time he was old enough to blow. He then went through all the business of being a choirboy and church organist, earning a scholarship from the Royal Academy of Music to study at the Conservatory of Leipzig: something that made him eminently qualified to write things like 'Tit-willow' and 'The flowers that bloom in the spring - tra-la'. Actually, before he did that he wrote incidental music to Shakespeare's play *The Tempest*, and this made quite an impression when it was performed at a Crystal Palace concert.

His connection with Shakespeare was a fruitful one. It was as a result of his incidental music to *The Merchant of Venice* in 1871 that he was invited to collaborate with the brilliant young librettist William Gilbert. The two became as inseparable as Laurel and Hardy, though it was a notoriously stormy relationship. Their first effort together was *Thespis*, or *The Gods Grown Old*, which didn't set the Thames on fire, but a few years later they hit the jackpot with *Trial by Jury*, and they were off and running with a series of 'comic operas' (their own preferred term) which are unequalled.

They produced one a year for twenty years in a theatre specially built for them by Richard D'Oyly Carte. The pieces were known as the 'Savoy Operas', and even though they were so often satirical of British social life of the day, they have remained fresh, vibrant and enormously popular. This is still as much due to the brilliance of Gilbert's words as to Sullivan's irresistible tunes and sophisticated scoring.

Sullivan was given all sorts of honours – doctorates from Oxford and Cambridge and a knighthood from Queen Victoria in 1883. Gilbert wasn't too pleased that he didn't get one at the same time, something that reminds me of when the great actor

Micheál Mac Líammóir got an honorary doctorate from UCD and his partner Hilton Edwards didn't. Hilton was known to have answered the phone and said, "No, Dr Mac Líammóir isn't in, but this is Nurse Edwards speaking."

Sullivan and Gilbert finally separated as the result of a silly quarrel about whether they could afford a new carpet for the Savoy Theatre. Silly or not, they wrote no more together and very little separately.

Sullivan did write a few more pieces for festivals and special occasions. He made a big effort in 1897 for Queen Victoria's Diamond Jubilee, producing the ballet *Victoria and Merrie England* and a festival *Te Deum*. In 1989 he struggled through the Leeds Festival performances of which he had been conductor for fifteen years. He was in great pain at the time, but for years he had been concealing the fact that he was suffering from a very painful malady. This had taken its toll on his constitution and, when he contracted a chill in 1900 he hadn't the strength to fight it off and died at the age of 58. A multitude of people lined the streets as he was brought to rest in St Paul's Cathedral.

Sullivan – A Middlebrow Mix

HMS Pinafore

Pinafore was the first worldwide success for Gilbert and Sullivan. It was produced in London in 1878 and ran for two years. It was soon produced in the USA as well, though at first without profit to its creators as no copyright laws protected them from the fast-buck merchants who pirated the work. Gilbert and Sullivan hastened to New York to stage the authentic version and protect their interests.

Pinafore was subtitled 'The Lass that Loved a Sailor' and the lass is Josephine, daughter of Captain Corcoran. She loves the lowly Ralph, but her father wants her to marry the admiral Sir Joseph Porter (an obvious tilt at Disraeli's First Lord of the Admiralty, W. H. Smith). It transpires that Corcoran and Ralph were mixed up as infants, so Corcoran is demoted to able seaman and Ralph becomes captain. This makes it all right for him to marry Josephine and everybody gets paired off very neatly – Sir Joseph with Hebe, one of his cousins.

Everybody has great numbers to sing. Sir Joseph tells us how he became First Lord without ever having gone to sea ('When I was a lad I served a term, as office boy in an attorney's firm'); Corcoran sings 'I am the captain of the Pinafore' and 'Fair moon to thee I sing', and also coins the catchphrase 'What, never? – hardly ever'; Mrs Cripps has 'I'm called little buttercup' and we mustn't forget the ensemble number 'Never mind the why and wherefore'. The overture was probably written by an assistant rather than Sullivan himself, and is a lively pot-pourri of all the best-known tunes.

The Pirates of Penzance

While in New York in 1879, Gilbert and Sullivan took the opportunity of premièring *The Pirates of Penzance* with the company already there for *Pinafore*. The London opening followed later.

Sullivan thought that, musically, *The Pirates* was infinitely superior in every way to *Pinafore* "tunier and more developed, of a higher class altogether". In the part of Mabel, the heroine, Sullivan poked fun at the florid manner of contemporary "serious" opera, and he was aided and abetted by Gilbert, who made fun of the high-flown melodramatic theatrical style. Mabel's song 'Poor wandering one' certainly puts any soprano's coloratura capabilities to the test.

There is no longer any copyright on the Gilbert and Sullivan operettas, so the strict rules laid down for their performance need not now be adhered to. *The Pirates* was a huge hit on Broadway twenty-odd years ago in a percussionised, brilliantly choreographed up-beat version. I had the thrill of playing the Sergeant of Police in a similar production in Dublin a little later. The Sergeant leads those two great numbers 'When the foeman bares his steel' and 'When a felon's not engaged in his employment'. More recently I played the Major-General, so had the opportunity of performing the celebrated tongue-twister 'I am the very model of a modern Major-General'.

I won't even attempt to summarise the plot, but it's all about the idiocy of blind devotion to duty, which accounts for the sub-title: 'The Slave of Duty.' It satirises the military and the police and has its quota of mock-patriotism (a recurrent theme with Gilbert and Sullivan). The pirates, who turn out to be noblemen, have great choruses, as have the Major-General's daughters and there are lovely tunes as well for the young lovers and even one which allows the Major-General to show off what voice he has ('Sighing softly to the river').

The Mikado

The Mikado, like most of the other Gilbert and Sullivan operettas, has a subtitle: 'The Town of Titipu'. This was the duo's biggest hit, running for 672 consecutive performances. It opened in 1885 at the Savoy Theatre.

This was the first G&S piece to be set in a foreign location, and was prompted by the 'Japanese Village' exhibition in Kensington and the fashion for all things Japanese. *The Mikado*, though, is not about ancient Japan but contemporary England, and again satirises English absurdities and the self-important characters (Lord High Everything Else) of English small-town life.

There are magnificent characters – the Mikado himself being one. He prides himself on his system of justice ('Let the punishment fit the crime'). Ko-Ko is a tailor who has become Lord High Executioner and has his 'little list' of society offenders who could be executed and never missed. He also has the celebrated 'Tit-Willow' song. Yum-Yum and Nanki-Poo are the young lovers who survive the dangers of decapitation and being buried alive to live happily ever after. Nanki-Poo arrives in Titipu declaring himself 'A wandering minstrel' and Yum-Yum with her friends Pitti-Sing and Peep-Bo are the 'Three little maids from school'. The list of hit numbers seems endless, from lyrical ones like 'The sun whose rays are all ablaze' to the catchy 'Flowers that bloom in the spring - tra-la!'

EDVARD GRIEG
(1843-1907)

Some of his fellow composers had harsh things to say about Grieg
– Debussy's opinion was that he was a "pink bon-bon wrapped
in sugar". Others, however, thought well of him. Liszt
championed his music and helped make a success of the 'Piano
Concerto in A Minor', which became one of the most frequently
played of all piano concertos.

Grieg was born in Bergen, Norway and studied at the
Leipzig Conservatory. From early on he wanted to be a 'national'
composer rather than merely a Norwegian imitator of the
Germans. He was eager to tap the source of Norwegian folk music
and to bring it to the attention of the world.

When Grieg was a boy his teachers forecast a brilliant future for him as a concert pianist but a breakdown from overwork,
complicated by pleurisy, left him with one lung and an accident
to one of his hands hampered his career as a pianist. He had to
settle for a quieter life of teaching and composing. He did tour
with his wife Nina Hagerup, who sang his songs enchantingly,
especially one which he dedicated to her – the beautiful 'I Love
You'. It was a happy marriage, marred by the tragedy of losing
their only daughter in her babyhood.

When he was only 31, Grieg was sufficiently well thought of
as a composer to be granted a life pension by the Norwegian
government. This financial security relieved him of the necessity
to write the large-scale works expected of the leading composers
of the day and to concentrate instead on the smaller forms in
which he excelled – particularly songs and piano pieces. He did
attempt one symphony early on but apart from that, the piano
concerto and the *Peer Gynt* music, most of the later orchestral
works are arrangements of piano pieces.

Grieg received honours and degrees from many countries
other than his own. Cambridge University made him a Doctor of
Music at the same time it honoured Tchaikovsky, Saint-Saëns and
Bruch.

George Bernard Shaw once called the composer "the infini-
tesimal Grieg", but this is only true in that his finest pieces are
romantic miniatures in a simple style derived from Norwegian
folk music. He did more to establish a Norwegian national style than

any of his countrymen. When he died in 1907 in his villa over-looking a fjord in Troldhaugen, his body lay in state, dozens of foreign governments participated in the funeral and hundreds of thousands of Norwegians lined the streets in tribute.

Grieg – A Middlebrow Mix

Piano Concerto in A Minor

One composition by Grieg stands out from all the others and is one of the most powerful of its kind. This is his one and only piano concerto, which was first performed in Copenhagen in 1869. The soloist was Edmund Neupart, who wrote to Grieg after the performance:

> On Saturday your divine concerto resounded in the great hall of the Casino. The triumph I achieved was tremendous. Even as early as the cadenza in the first movement the public broke into a real storm.

He went on to say that the critic Rubinstein had expressed himself astounded to have heard a work of such genius. For the Norwegians it has become something of a national monument and is played at a special concert every year with celebrated soloists of every nationality being invited to give their interpretation.

Grieg frequently performed the piano concerto himself. He revised the score prior to its publication in 1872 and continued to make changes both in the solo part and the orchestrations up to the time of his death. It is certainly a vehicle for virtuosic display, but it is rich in melody and the lyrical genius which was the hallmark of the composer is never submerged.

The concerto opens with a quiet drum roll which increases in volume until it explodes into a dramatic chord from piano and orchestra. Out of this emerges the lovely theme, first stated by woodwinds and then taken up by the piano. The music unfolds with increasing passion until we reach the cadenza, a rhapsodic interlude which is a tour de force for the soloist. The second movement is an intermezzo-like adagio – sad and tranquil. The finale, based on the halling (a characteristic Norwegian dance), starts off vigorously and exuberantly but Grieg has not run out of melody. He has reserved one of his best wines for last and we are allowed to wallow in it before the vitality reasserts itself and a powerful drum roll heralds the triumphant climax.

Peer Gynt Suite Nos. 1 and 2

The best known of Grieg's orchestral works are the two suites he developed from 22 pieces of incidental music for Henrik Ibsen's play *Peer Gynt*. Ibsen based his hero on a real character who lived in Norway at the beginning of the 19th century – he was a peasant, an inveterate boaster and a liar.

Grieg himself was not too happy about *Peer Gynt* at the time of composition. He complained of having to do "patchwork" since the theatrical management had dictated the duration of each musical selection as well as its position in the overall design. However, Grieg produced some remarkable pieces. Four of them make up the first and by far the most popular of the orchestral suites: 'Morning', which depicts a beautiful rising sun; 'Aase's Death', emotional and melancholy; 'Anitra's Dance', with its rhythmic gaiety and the dramatic 'In the Hall of the Mountain King', which is probably the most familiar piece of music he ever wrote. In fact it was so much associated with him that he came to feel about it much as Rachmaninov did about his 'Prelude in C Sharp Minor' or Judy Garland about 'Somewhere Over the Rainbow'. Miss Garland was once quoted as saying that she felt "up to my ass in rainbows". The best known number in the second orchestral suite is 'Solveig's Song', which Grieg did actually like himself – it has a wonderful melody and is a great favourite in both its vocal and instrumental versions.

Norwegian Dances and Symphonic Dances

There are four of each – all originally written for piano duet and then orchestrated. Derived from Norwegian folk music, they are gay and colourful – the Norwegian counterpart to Dvorák's 'Slavonic Dances'.

The Holberg Suite

'The Holberg Suite' was originally written by Grieg for piano, but he later scored it for strings and this is the version we usually hear. It was intended to commemorate the bicentenary of the birth of Ludwig Holberg – a Norwegian-born poet and playwright. Grieg laid out the suite in the form prevalent in Holberg's time – a prelude and four dances.

Songs

'Ich Liebe Dich' ('I Love You') is the best known. Two others, 'Heart's Wound' and 'Last Spring' were plaintively orchestrated as 'Two Elegiac Melodies'.

Lyric Pieces

There are altogether 69 lyric pieces for piano. Some of the best known are 'Butterflies', 'Lonely wanderer', 'March of the dwarfs' and 'Wedding day at Troldhaugen'. Some of the pieces were orchestrated to make up the 'Lyric Suite'.

NICOLAI RIMSKY-KORSAKOV
(1844-1908)

Nicolai Rimsky-Korsakov was a Russian aristocrat whose family wanted him to be a naval officer. At the age of twelve he went to a naval academy and later spent six years at sea. He had shown musical talent, though, and when he was 21 he began to take music seriously. He met Balakirev, leader of the 'Mighty Five', who suggested that he write a symphony. "No bother," said Rimsky, even though he had no knowledge of harmony, counterpoint or orchestration. He started work, but was called away to sea and didn't complete his symphony until his return two and a half years later.

By pulling strings with the Minister for the Marine, Rimsky-Korsakov was able to put active service behind him and accept the civilian post of inspector of the music bands of the Navy Department. Then, at the age of 27, on the strength of a few compositions, he was appointed Professor of Composition at the St Petersburg Conservatory. He must have been the bluffer of all time, because he didn't mind admitting later that he was probably the most ignorant professor ever to grace the academy. However, he was industrious and conscientious, he studied hard, and by the time he was 30 he was the most learned professor in Russia.

Rimsky-Korsakov outgrew the school of Balakirev and became the leader of a new group consisting of his own pupils. Everyone wanted to study with him, and he came to be seen as the fountain of all musical knowledge. He studied each musical instrument intently, learning its range and capabilities. This resulted in him becoming known as the "incomparable master of orchestration". He also devoted countless hours to polishing and finishing the works of his friends – particularly those of Mussorgsky, who found it difficult to finish anything.

After hearing Wagner's *Ring* in 1889, Rimsky-Korsakov determined to concentrate on writing opera, eventually completing more than a dozen. He himself considered his operatic output to be the most important part of his work. However, I don't think any of them are still performed or have even been recorded. The only way these operas are remembered is through the orchestral suites.

Rimsky-Korsakov will always be remembered for his

orchestral music and for the great influence he had on other composers. One scribe commented on his "brilliant and daring harmony, extraordinary talent for instrumentation, dazzling combination of colours and, rare among Russian composers, sunshine and warmth". That about sums up the characteristics of this Russian master, who died of a heart attack in his mid-sixties.

Rimsky-Korsakov – A Middlebrow Mix

Scheherezade (symphonic suite)

The story of this great symphonic suite was drawn from the Arabian Nights, and more specifically *The Thousand and One Nights*, in which Scheherezade is the storytelling heroine. It is concerned with the powerful Sultan Schariar who, convinced of women's unfaithfulness, puts all his wives to death after their wedding night. Scheherezade saves herself by spinning colourful yarns which stretch over a thousand and one nights in the telling, and so intrigued is the Sultan that he spares her life.

Each of the four movements in the suite has a descriptive title and contains a voluptuous melody on solo violin, representing Scheherezade, and a stern theme depicting the all-powerful Sultan. The first movement is 'The Sea and Sinbad's Ship', a mighty seascape which conjures up a vision of Sinbad on the deck of his ship riding out the swells. Then comes 'The Tale of the Kalendar Prince', a land-based adventure with warlike sounds. The 'Young Prince and the Young Princess' is a tender romance and, finally, we have 'The Festival at Baghdad – the Sea-Shipwreck on a Rock Surmounted by a Bronze Warrior'. That's quite a mouthful, and indeed it contains wild revels and the return of the sea music of the first movement. This time a storm rages and the ship is wrecked on the craggy rocks over which watches the legendary figure of the Bronze Warrior: but it's only a story and the gentle Scheherezade has the last word, bringing comfort to the wise King who has spared her life.

Scheherezade is recognised as one of the great descriptive works, a masterpiece of 'programme music'. Rimsky-Korsakov spent some years in the navy, so his impressions of the sea are first-hand. Orchestration became his passion, and the work shows why such adjectives have been applied to it as "picturesque", "imaginative", "colourful" and "vivid". He was the master of instrumentation.

Capriccio Espagnol ('Spanish Caprice')

This is another big orchestral work in five movements to which all the adjectives of the "colourful" variety also apply. It was written in 1887 and based on Spanish folk tunes. There are prominent solo parts for violin, harp, and clarinet, and the castanets help to give it a tremendous *joie de vivre* or should I say "alegría"?

Suite from *The Tale of Tsar Saltan*

This, believe it or not, is the abbreviated title of the opera – well, you could hardly expect people to call it (as the composer did) *The Tale of Tsar Saltan, of his son the famous and mighty hero Prince Guidon Saltanovich and of the beautiful Swan Princess*. One of the amazing things that happens to Guidon is that he is turned into a bee, in which guise he takes pleasure in stinging his evil aunts. Yes! This is the opera that owes its fame to 'The flight of the bumble bee' which, of course has often been spoonerised into 'The bum of the flightle bee': though I prefer the musician's version, 'The blight of the humble fee'.

Suite from *The Golden Cockerel*

Another fairytale opera about a stupid Tsar and the ridiculous goings-on at his imaginary court. It was construed by the government of the day (1907) as a satire on Imperial Russia and performance was forbidden. Rimsky-Korsakov died the following year without ever hearing it. The most famous piece is the lovely 'Hymn to the sun', but the whole orchestral suite is well worth hearing. Particularly noteworthy is the tremendous processional march in the final movement.

GABRIEL FAURÉ
(1845-1924)

It will surprise some that Gabriel Fauré gets into the Top 40, but the fact is that we hear more music by Fauré on *Music for Middle-brows* than by some of his more distinguished countrymen. He produced a large quantity of delightful light music and, had he not lived a long life, would still be regarded as a composer of easygoing, tuneful trifles. These include 'The Dolly Suite', 'Pavane' and the charming suite 'Masques et Bergamasques'. Until he was in his sixties, Fauré specialised in the smaller forms of composition – incidental music to plays, piano pieces and songs. His songs are so highly regarded that he has been called "the French Schubert".

Later in life Fauré turned his hand to compositions on a larger scale – song cycles, big chamber works and an opera based on Homer's *Odyssey*. He wrote no symphonies or concertos and few orchestral works of any size.

By the time he was eight Fauré had shown enough musical promise for his father to send him from his home town of Parmiers to study in Paris. The director of the famous École Niedermayer was so impressed by the boy's organ-playing – largely self-taught – that he offered him a full scholarship. One of his teachers was Saint-Saëns, who became a close friend, introduced him to poets and other musicians and helped him to get jobs. Fauré held various posts as a church organist, culminating in the sinecure of the Madeleine Church in Paris (Saint-Saëns had himself held this post as a much younger man).

Fauré was an industrious teacher – first of all at the École Niedermayer and then at the Paris Conservatoire, where he was director from 1905 to 1920. Among the people who benefited from his teaching were the Romanian composer Georges Enesco, the celebrated teacher Nadia Boulanger and Maurice 'Bolero' Ravel. Fauré lived long enough to see great changes in musical styles. His own style did not change – he remained primarily a late-Romantic of the 19th century. However, he was a tolerant, open-minded man and was quite happy to encourage the 'new music' of those like Ravel and the impressionism of Debussy.

Fauré was a gentle, kindly man and he deservedly received a number of honours. He was made a member of the Academie, a commander of the Légion d'Honneur and, a year before his death, president of the Paris section of the International Society of Contemporary Music. Early in his seventies he began to experience symptoms of deafness. He managed to conceal this for a few years, but finally had to step down from his Conservatoire post in 1920. He died four years later.

Gabriel Fauré's music is not as well known outside France as that of his teacher Saint-Saëns or his pupil Ravel, but I love the description I came across of him as:

> *The classic example of a rare, virtually priceless wine that simply refuses to travel.*

Fauré – A Middlebrow Mix

Fauré is included not because he wrote any monumental works but because instead he was the composer of so many tuneful smaller pieces. One of his biggest works was the *Requiem*, one of the best loved of all choral works. The music is quiet, reflective, in total contrast to, say, Verdi's opera-like *Requiem*. If you don't feel like going for the work in toto, pick out the 'Pie Jesu' for solo treble.

Outstanding among Fauré's shorter pieces are 'Pavane', a lovely piece scored for flute with plucked string accompaniment but sometimes heard in a choral arrangement (this was rather strangely chosen as the theme tune of the World Cup 1998); 'Aprés Un Rêve' ('After a Dream'), probably Fauré's most popular song but also available in arrangements for other instruments, notably the cello.

Two suites should be mentioned: 'The Dolly Suite', written for piano duet but later orchestrated for a ballet and 'Masques et Bergamasques', a delightful four-movement orchestral suite – unpretentious, tuneful with a gem of an overture.

EDWARD ELGAR
(1857-1934)

Edward Elgar, the pride and joy of England, was largely a self-made man. It is true that he was brought up in an atmosphere of music, his father being an organist who also ran a music shop. However, young Edward attended no great conservatoires and had no great names among his teachers. He applied himself to playing piano, organ, violin, cello, double-bass, bassoon and trombone, taking part in all the local music-making around his home area of Worcester. He took on the jobs of bandmaster of the county mental home and conductor of the Worcester Orchestral Society and played violin in a Birmingham orchestra. All this gave him a great knowledge of instrumentation and his name began to appear as composer on the concert programmes of all the musical organisations.

Elgar's life as a composer started in earnest with his marriage in 1889. He married one of his pupils, Caroline Roberts, who was eight years his senior. She was a strong personality – the daughter of a Major-General – and had great faith in her husband's capabilities. Success did not come immediately, however. A spell in London failed to set society alight but, back in Worcestershire, Elgar took advantage of the English festival system and composed a number of the choral-orchestral works which became his trademark. Then, in 1899, came the 'Enigma Variations', which catapulted him into the first rank of composers and he never looked back.

Someone once said that Elgar, typical English gentleman that he was, wrote "the sort of music that gives the composer the degree of Doctor of Music from an English university". Elgar got a lot more than a DMus. He was knighted in 1904, received the Order of Merit in 1911, became Master of the King's Music in 1924 and was created a baronet in 1931. His beloved wife, his great inspiration, died in 1920, a cruel blow from which he never properly recovered. He lived in semi-retirement in the county of his birth for the remaining fourteen years of his life.

Elgar was the man for the big occasion. He was the one called upon to provide stirring tunes for the pageants and musical events such as coronations, state visits and grand openings. He was very much into the pomp and circumstance though, strangely, he was not a good mixer.

He loved the outdoors, and retained a boyish enthusiasm for fishing, walking, riding, cycling and, later, motoring. He was also a great racegoer and punter – during his affluent days he kept a separate race-going bank account. Professionally he was inclined to stand on his dignity and most of his colleagues found him aloof and stand-offish. He is best remembered for the ceremonial pieces, but there is a lot more to him than that. His music did not travel well – it appealed more to his countrymen, who found in it exactly what they wanted. Grove says of him that:

> They found in Elgar a new Handel but a Handel who happened to be an Englishman born and bred.

Elgar – A Middlebrow Mix

The Enigma Variations

The 'Enigma Variations' first established Edward Elgar as a composer of the first rank. The first performance was given in 1899 when Elgar was 42 years of age. The official title of the work is 'Variations on an Original Theme' and to quote the composer:

> *In this music I have sketched, for their amusement and mine, the idiosyncrasies of thirteen of my friends...the variations should stand simply as a piece of music, the enigma I will not explain. Its dark saying must be left unguessed.*

It was only after Elgar's death that the identities of his friends were revealed. The best known variation is the ninth, known as 'Nimrod'. It is the musical portrait of A. J. Jaeger, then a member of the publishing firm of Novello. Jaeger is German for 'hunter' and Nimrod was the mighty Biblical hunter.

This variation is often played on its own and deserves to be: there are few if any more sonorous pieces of music written by an Englishman. There is another enigma attached to this work. Elgar suggested that there was a secret or hidden theme running throughout but this has never been identified. I did some research to see if the first performance was on 1 April, but no! Still, I think all the speculation has given Sir Edward a quiet chuckle in his resting place.

Salut d'Amour ('Love's Greeting')

Elgar composed this morsel in 1889 for his newly born daughter Carice and sold the copyright for two guineas. It haunted him ever after, as it became his most played piece and earned a fortune for the publisher. Two other pieces for small orchestra composed around the same time are 'Chanson de Matin' ('Morning Song') and 'Chanson de Soir' ('Evening Song'). They weren't published until a good deal later, by which time Elgar had made his name. They are both delicate miniatures which were immediately taken to the hearts of English concert-goers.

Pomp and Circumstance Marches

The word 'circumstance', as used by Shakespeare means pageantry and ceremony and there is plenty of that in Elgar's music. He hoped that these five marches would serve as reminders of England's greatness. 'March No. 1' is the most celebrated because it has the tune to which the English lustily sing 'Land of Hope and Glory' at every opportunity. The last night of each season's Prom concerts at the Royal Albert Hall in London is a well-known opportunity. 'March No. 4' also has a theme which gained the status of a national song during World War II. Sir Alan Herbert wrote the words for 'Song of Freedom' which has the opening line 'All men must be free'.

Cello Concerto in E Minor

This concerto could in some sense be considered Elgar's swansong. It was composed and first performed under his direction in 1919, fifteen years before he died but only a few months before the death of his wife, which almost silenced him completely. It's a heart-rending piece with at least one memorable melody. Indeed it is, I suppose, Elgar's 'Pathétique', as if, like Tchaikovsky, he was prophesying doom.

It's ironic too, that in our time, the concerto has been associated with tragedy, being indelibly linked with the British cellist Jacqueline du Pré; its popularity in the last 35 years has been due to its association with her. Du Pré was a brilliant, life-loving musician married to the pianist and conductor Daniel Barenboim. She contracted multiple sclerosis, which destroyed her musical ability and died in 1987 at the age of 42. You must listen to her recording of the Elgar concerto with the London Symphony Orchestra conducted by Sir John Barbirolli.

The Dream of Gerontius

This may not be one of the all-time great oratorios, but there was a big vogue for it when I was growing up and it was nearly as much a favourite with Our Lady's Choral Society as Handel's *Messiah*. I remember hearing it with Sir John Barbirolli conducting (he seemed to have a great affinity with the music of Elgar).

Gerontius is a setting of a poem by Cardinal Newman and though one criticism was that "it stinks of incense", it is a deeply felt work with many marvellous moments for the three solo singers and the chorus. Many consider it to be Elgar's masterpiece and, unlike many of his other works, it has been widely acclaimed.

GIACOMO PUCCINI
(1858-1924)

After Verdi, Puccini was certainly "the man" for Italian opera – with Rossini, Donizetti and Bellini coming in some yards behind. Puccini did not toss off operas with great facility, he worked slowly and painstakingly, and there was usually a gap of a few years between each of them. He wrote tear-jerkers with broad, luscious melodies, and three of his operas – *La Bohème*, *Tosca* and *Madam Butterfly* are among the most popular of all time.

Puccini was born into a musical family in the town of Lucca, Italy and from an early age he received training as a church musician. However, he was 22 before a grant from Queen Margherita of Italy enabled him to go to the Milan Conservatory. Here he studied with Ponchielli of *La Gioconda* fame. His first couple of attempts at opera-writing were unsuccessful, but then came *Manon Lescaut*, followed at intervals by the Big Three, establishing him as the leading Italian composer of his generation.

The success of the operas also earned him a fortune and he was able to buy a lakeside estate near his native town. He spent a lot of time here indulging his passion for hunting wildfowl and driving his new-fangled motor car. He also undertook a number of promotional tours in order to launch his works on the international stage.

After *Madam Butterfly*, Puccini found it increasingly difficult to find subjects and dramatic settings to compare with bohemian Paris in the 1830s, revolutionary Rome in 1800 and Japan in the early-20th century. He finally chose the California Gold Rush of 1849 and came up with *The Girl of the Golden West*. He went to New York to supervise the productions at the Metropolitan Opera in 1910 and greatly enjoyed the lavish American hospitality.

Puccini's last opera was *Turandot*, the exotic tale of a Chinese princess. It remained unfinished when he died of throat cancer in 1924. Mussolini had made him a member of the Italian Senate, and when he died gave him a magnificent state funeral of the sort usually reserved for top-ranking statesmen rather than composers.

Puccini – A Middlebrow Mix

La Bohème

Puccini had had some success with *Manon Lescaut* in 1893 but it was *La Bohème* that really cemented his international reputation. It was premièred in 1896 with the 29-year-old Arturo Toscanini conducting.

The setting is Paris in the 1840s. Two impecunious artists, Rodolfo (a poet) and Marcello (a painter) live in a bohemian garret. Occupying an attic in the same house is a seamstress, Mimi, who shyly knocks on the men's door to ask for a light for her candle. Finding Rodolfo alone, she introduces herself and they fall head over heels in love. However, it soon becomes apparent that Mimi is not a well girl, she is suffering from the dreaded consumption, much to the anxiety of Rodolfo. Running parallel with this love story is the volatile relationship between Marcello and Musetta, which provides some moments of light relief, but it is the tragedy that prevails. Poor Mimi is too weak to survive – she gently drifts off into unconsciousness, which turns out to be permanent, leaving Rodolfo in despair.

The meeting between Mimi and Rodolfo in Act I gives rise to the tenor aria 'Che gelida manina' ('Your tiny hand is frozen'); and the soprano's 'Mi chiamo Mimi' ('My name is Mimi') and the glorious duet ending the act, 'O soave fanciulla' ('O lovely maid in the moonlight'). Outstanding in Act II is Musetta's waltz song 'Quando m'en vo'. In Act IV Rodolfo and Marcello have the great duet 'O Mimi, tu piu non torni' ('Mimi, false one') and finally comes the great death scene duet between the ill-fated lovers.

Tosca

This great work followed four years after *La Bohème*. It took Puccini time to complete things because he was constantly interrupted – often to go to some far-flung place to supervise a new production of a previous success. He was also thorough in his research. For *Tosca* he was careful to check religious details and took a trip to Rome to check the sound of church bells from the heights of the Castello Sant'Angelo.

The action takes place in Rome in 1800. Tosca is a singer

who is in love with the painter Cavaradossi, who has promised
to help his friend Angelotti, a political offender, to escape from
Rome. Scarpia, the chief of police, is the villain of the piece and
causes grief to them all. He hunts Angelotti, tortures Cavaradossi
to get him to reveal his friend's hiding place and forces his attentions on Tosca. Scarpia gets his just deserts as Tosca stabs and
kills him but Cavaradossi dies too. Scarpia has promised that his
execution will be faked, but the bullets are all too real. Tosca, in
the tradition of all great tragedies, prefers to follow her lover
into death and she flings herself from the battlements.

Act I has the great tenor aria 'Recondita armonia'.
Cavardossi muses over his painting of the Madonna in which he
sees the face of his beloved Tosca. The big number in Act II is
'Vissi d'arte', a despairing aria sung by Tosca when she is in the
clutches of the wicked Scarpia. All she ever wanted, she says,
was to live for her art. Cavaradossi has another wonderful aria
in Act III, 'E lucevan le stelle' ('The stars shine brightly'). He is in
prison awaiting his final hour and is overcome by memories of
Tosca and thoughts of his approaching death.

Madam Butterfly

Four years after *Tosca* came this tragic tale of the Japanese girl
Cio-Cio-San. She has every faith in the American lieutenant
Pinkerton, who calls her his 'butterfly'. She also believes that
their 'marriage' is binding, but he has other ideas. He sails for
America and she waits for him in Nagasaki where she bears his
child. Three years later he returns but is accompanied by his
American bride. This is too much for Butterfly to bear and, in
traditional Japanese fashion, she falls on her father's sword.

Puccini saw David Belasco's play *Madam Butterfly* in London in 1900 and was attracted not only by the oriental setting of
the drama but by the musical possibilities suggested by it. His
plan was to explore the contrast between European and Oriental values, with one act set in North America and another in
Japan. This idea was dropped in favour of a scene at the American consulate, but this, in turn, was dropped and he concentrated on Butterfly and on the Japanese setting.

The première at La Scala in 1904 was a resounding failure
and Puccini continued to tinker with the opera for some time
afterwards, principally adding new material for Pinkerton in Act

II. Since then, of course, *Madam Butterfly* has become one of the world's most popular operas. It is a tribute to Puccini and the power of the music that we even accept Western sopranos of enormous proportions in the role of the delicate Cio-Cio-San.

Act I ends with the marvellous love duet 'Viene la sera', with Pinkerton and Butterfly enchanted with each other. Act II is full of wonderful numbers, including the celebrated soprano aria 'Un bel di'. Butterfly describes her dream of Pinkerton's return 'one fine day'. Then we have the 'Flower duet' and the lovely 'Humming chorus'. Pinkerton's ship has been spotted coming into the harbour. In the stillness of the night Butterfly waits, while the humming voices can be heard in the distance.

Turandot

Turandot was not quite finished when Puccini died in 1924. Franco Alfano later put the finishing touches to it, but first the incomplete version was performed under Toscanini. When he had played the last notes composed by Puccini, he laid down his baton, turned to the audience, and said, "At this point the master laid down his pen."

The action takes place in ancient Peking. Princess Turandot has decreed that she will marry any prince who can solve three riddles but that anyone who fails in his attempt will be executed. Many have tried, all have failed. A mysterious prince, however, gives the correct answers. Turandot is distraught, as she has taken a vow to remain a virgin so Calaf (that's who he is) gives her a chance to get out of the bargain. If she can discover his name by daybreak, he will pay the forfeit and die; if not, she will be his. There is a big love scene, after which Calaf tells Turandot his name, thus placing his life in her hands. Fortunately he doesn't suffer the same fate as Samson when he gave Delilah his secret. Turandot announces that his name is Love and all join in the rejoicing (all, that is, except poor Liu, a slave girl, who has killed herself rather than betray her beloved master Prince Calaf).

There are some well-known arias such as 'Signore Ascolta', in which Liu pleads with Calaf not to take on the challenge of the three riddles; 'In questa reggia' Turandot explains that her vow to remain pure has been inspired by an ancient princess who was cruelly betrayed by a man but all pale into insignificance in comparison to 'Nessun dorma'. This is the most popular tenor aria of all time – at least since the 1994 World Cup when Pavarotti became the idol of football fans the world over. Since then, it has become a must for every tenor who half fancies himself as a 'can belto'. For the record, it comes at the beginning of Act III as Calaf lyrically contemplates his coming victory over the princess who has decreed that 'none shall sleep' until his name has been discovered.

Gianni Schicchi

This is one of a trio of one-act operas which were performed together at the Metropolitan Opera in New York in 1919. This one has to be mentioned because of the aria 'O mio babbino caro' ('O my beloved father') which is a great favourite with sopranos and listeners. In my youth the New Zealand soprano Joan Hammond (not to be confused with the Australian Joan Sutherland) was particularly associated with it. It is a comic opera, but this is a serious aria in which the heroine begs her father to let her marry her young lover.

OTHER LATE-ROMANTIC NOTEWORTHIES

Emil Waldteufel
(1837-1915)

Waldteufel was born in Strasbourg on the Franco-German bor-
der, and came from a very musical family – his father and many
of his relations were musicians, but Emil really outshone them
all. He toured the capitals of Europe with an orchestra which
played his own tunes, and became known as "the French
Strauss".

It's easy for us to see that Waldteufel was less versatile, less
inventive than his Viennese counterpart but he certainly had a
great melodic gift. Of his several hundred waltz and other dance
tunes, 'The Skaters' is still one of the best loved. Like the Strauss
waltzes, it consists of not a single but a whole sequence of charming melodies. Another very popular one is 'Estudiantina', but he
can't claim the credit for the tune in this case, it's a waltz version
of Chabrier's *España*.

Max Bruch
(1838-1920)

Max Bruch is well known to us for his 'Violin Concerto in G
Minor', and particularly for its slow movement, an adagio which
is one of the most beautiful ever penned for the violin.

Bruch's mother was a gifted singer and Max showed great
musical promise at an early age. He was born in Cologne and
started composing when he was only nine. He was fourteen
when he won the Mozart Scholarship in Frankfurt which gave
him four years of study with distinguished pedagogues (posh
word for teachers).

The 'Concerto in G Minor' is one of the most popular of all
violin concertos. Bruch made his first sketches for it when he
was just nineteen, but did not complete the score until about ten
years later. He did not play the violin himself, but he had lots of
advice from the renowned Joseph Joachim, to whom the concerto
was dedicated and who gave it its first formal presentation in
1868. It was another nine years before London was to hear the
concerto, when the great Spanish virtuoso Pablo de Sarasate

introduced it to the British public. It was undoubtedly Joachim
who prevailed on Bruch to introduce an element of virtuosity
into the concerto, but it is essentially lyrical throughout, with an
adagio that has been described as "one of the melodic glories of
the 19th century". In the outer movements, particularly the rondo
finale, the violin is allowed a certain amount of flamboyance,
but lyricism is never far away. Bruch certainly knew how to get
the instrument to sing.

Bruch was not Jewish, though it is sometimes presumed that
he was because of his great interest in traditional Jewish melodies. However, he was also drawn to the folk music of Scotland,
Wales and his own native Germany.

Bruch married a singer in 1881 and two years later he went
on a tour to America. On his return he undertook the direction
of the Orchestral Society at Breslau, and held that post for seven
years – longer than most of his other tenures. He had many honours and decorations bestowed upon him, including honorary
degrees from the universities of Cambridge, Breslau and Berlin.
For the last ten years of his life he lived quietly in retirement near
Berlin and died there in 1920.

Pablo de Sarasate
(1844-1908)

The Spanish composer Sarasate was the direct successor of
Paganini as the most spectacular violin virtuoso of his time.
Sarasate had small hands and could not manage the immense
stretches required by Paganini's music, so he wrote pieces himself with which he could dazzle audiences in his own way. Those
pieces certainly make high musical demands, but for violinists
who are merely human they are more manageable than some of
Paganini's.

Sarasate was a contemporary of that other great violinist
Joseph Joachim, but the Spaniard was much more popular as a
recitalist because he was more of an entertainer. Like Kreisler
later on, Sarasate played a lot of lightweight pieces, but played
them with such grace and polish that they were a joy to hear.
He played the larger works as well, of course. Lalo composed his
violin concerto and 'Symphonie Espagnole' especially for him,
and Saint-Saëns his 'First' and 'Third' concertos.

Sarasate himself wrote romances, fantasies and, especially, transcriptions of Spanish airs and dances. His four books of Spanish dances are among the most popular violin solos in existence. Another must is the 'Carmen Fantasy' – a brilliant set of variations for solo violin and orchestra of all the well-known tunes from Bizet's opera. Perhaps his most popular piece of all is 'Zigeunerweisen' ('Gypsy Airs') a brilliant work in the style of a Hungarian rhapsody.

Charles Widor
(1844-1937)

After the death of Bach in 1750, very little organ music of major significance was written for a century or so. But then in the mid-19th century came a great resurgence of activity among composer-organists in France. This was led by César Franck and among those who followed, an outstanding figure was Widor. He lived to the age of 93 and his works include ten 'symphonies' for organ solo.

The term 'symphony' is sometimes inappropriate for these organ works, as they can have six or seven movements of quite short duration. However, it is justified in the treatment of the organ as a sort of self-contained orchestra. The later ones in particular make great demands on the resources of both player and instrument. Widor was an innovator and contributed greatly to the development of organ technique and variety of sound.

He has other works to his credit – orchestral, operatic, chamber music – but is particularly known to middlebrows for one piece: the Toccata from 'Organ Symphony No. 5'. This has become a hugely popular showpiece, rivalling Bach's 'Toccata and Fugue in D Minor' and is a thrilling kaleidoscope of sound.

Christian Sinding
(1856-1941)

Norwegian Christian Sinding had a long life, he was 85 when he died in 1941. His compositions are many and varied, but the one everyone knows is the piano piece which, during my formative years anyway, was an essential part of every pianist's repertoire – 'The Rustle of Spring'. There is a lovely tune in the left hand, while the right hand has cascades of rippling notes and the whole thing is a charming and entertaining party piece.

Ruggiero Leoncavallo
(1857-1919)

Leoncavallo was one of the one-work wonders. He was six years older than Mascagni, but took longer to reach celebrity status. He was born in Naples and studied at the Conservatory there but went through a bad time after that until he came up with *I Pagliacci* when he was 35.

This was modelled on Mascagni's *Cavalleria Rusticana* and exploited the existing trend for verismo opera, the musical counterpart of literary realism. The successful première in 1892 with Toscanini conducting made Leoncavallo famous overnight. *I Pagliacci* was staged by New York's Metropolitan Opera in 1893 as a double-bill with *Cavalleria Rusticana* and the twins 'Cav and Pag' have been almost inseparable ever since.

Fame, however, did not ensure a trouble-free ride for Leoncavallo. An earlier opera of his was staged and was a failure, and then he had the audacity to take on Puccini in head-to-head combat with his version of *La Bohème*. The two worked on the subject simultaneously, but Puccini got there first and Leoncavallo's opera, premièred a year later, never posed a serious threat. He wasn't a bit pleased, accusing Puccini of plagiarism, but it was obviously a case of sour grapes.

In 1906 Leoncavallo toured the USA and Canada, again following in Mascagni's footsteps, and here he first turned his hand to operetta. He had a natural aptitude for lighter music and his great song 'Mattinata' was first recorded by Caruso in 1904. Leoncavallo had an intense desire to be taken seriously as a composer, but just as 'Cav and Pag' will always be linked, so will their composers as the two who never managed to repeat their one great success.

The story of *I Pagliacci* takes place in a village in southern Italy in 1865. In the famous Prologue, Tonio alerts the audience that they are to see a drama taken from real life. A company of strolling players arrive and are greeted by the villagers.

The players are Canio (tenor), his wife Nedda (soprano), Tonio (baritone) who is deformed and Beppe (tenor). Nedda falls for a handsome villager Silvio (baritone) and repulses the advances of Tonio. Enraged, Tonio helps Canio to surprise his wife and her lover, but Silvio escapes unrecognised and Nedda refuses to identify him.

In the second act the players perform their comedy – a story which parallels their actual situation. Canio confuses play and reality and demands in vain from his wife the name of her lover. Losing all control he stabs Nedda to death. Silvio, who is in the audience, rushes to the stage in a vain attempt to save Nedda and is himself killed by the demented Canio.

The prologue is a great baritone showpiece, and in the aria 'Vesti la guibba' ('On with the motley') Canio paints his face and puts on his clown's costume, even though his heart is breaking.

Emil von Reznicek
(1860-1945)

The Austrian composer Reznicek, who died at a great age in 1945, held a number of posts as conductor of theatre orchestras and military bands. As a composer he was drawn towards the dramatic side of music and his greatest theatrical success came in 1894 when the comic opera *Donna Diana* was written within a few weeks and shown for the first time in Prague.

The scene is set in the castle of Don Diego at Barcelona during the period of Catalan independence. I doubt if the opera is ever performed nowadays but I just had to include Reznicek because of the overture, which is one of the brightest and most delightful you are ever likely to hear.

Gustav Mahler
(1860-1911)

By the age of 25, Mahler was one of the leading opera conductors of the day. He was director of the Vienna Court Opera for ten years, where he ruled with a baton of iron. Later he was principal conductor at the Metropolitan in New York for some time.

He never wrote an opera of his own, but poured all his emotions into his symphonies. He wrote the magic number of nine (the tenth was unfinished). These are monumental works, some requiring huge orchestral forces and voices as well. He himself once said that a symphony "should contain the world". I would write a lot more about Mahler's symphonies (others have), but they aren't really middlebrow. 'Symphony No. 1' is probably the most accessible because of its folksong melodies, but the adagietto from 'Symphony No. 5' is the most familiar piece because of its use in Visconti's film *Death in Venice*.

Gustave Charpentier
(1860-1956)

French composer Charpentier must rank with Sibelius as one of the longest-lived of all – he died in 1956 at the age of 95. Unfortunately, Charpentier didn't fill all those years with memorable compositions, in fact he's really known only for one, the opera *Louise*, which has one very popular aria, 'Depuis le jour'.

A young dressmaker in Paris in 1900 is torn between her love for a poet (and attraction for his bohemian way of life) and her loyalty to her devoted but narrow-minded parents. The aria has a beautiful, sustained melody which lets the soprano show the quality of tone of her voice rather than indulge in vocal gymnastics so beloved of the divas. Charpentier was greatly concerned about the lack of opportunities for underprivileged girls in the Paris of his day, founding an institution where they could learn to sing, dance and act, and possibly find a career on the stage.

Pietro Mascagni
(1863-1945)

Pietro Mascagni has always been known as a one-work wonder, though he wasn't a bit pleased about that. He was determined to study music in spite of family opposition and was financed by an uncle. One of his teachers at the Milan Conservatory was Ponchielli of *La Gioconda* fame. Mascagni didn't last long at the conservatory but left to become conductor of a travelling opera company.

Then he got married and settled down as a small-town piano teacher. However, fame was just around the corner. Unknown to Mascagni, his wife entered *Cavalleria Rusticana* in a competition for one-act operas and it was awarded first prize. (I am reminded of the time when my daughter won a violin competition which she didn't want to enter. Unknown to her, her father had sent off a tape!)

Mascagni became an overnight celebrity and his opera was soon heard in theatres all over the world. It established the vogue for verismo and was embraced by composers like Leoncavallo, Puccini, Giordano and Cilea. Their subjects were taken from everyday life instead of the history and mythology which had been favoured by Rossini, Verdi and Wagner.

Anticipation was, of course, great for Mascagni's next work, but *L'Amico Fritz* didn't come up to expectations, though it had some great numbers which are still heard these days. However hard he tried over the next decade, the success of *Cavalleria* eluded him. He wrote about fifteen operas and even tried giving the premières of some outside Italy, but fared no better. However, he did become director of the Conservatory at Pesaro until extended leaves of absence for overseas tours cost him the job. In 1929 he succeeded Arturo Toscanini as musical director of La Scala in Milan. This appointment could mainly be put down to his opportunism in identifying with fascism. He had no scruples about beginning performances with the fascist hymn. He didn't long survive the collapse of fascism, dying in an obscure Roman hotel in 1945 at the age of 82.

Cavalleria Rusticana is set in a Sicilian village on Easter morning. The young soldier Turiddu (tenor) has returned from the army and seduced Santuzza (soprano), who is now pregnant by him and loves him sincerely. However, Turiddu takes up with his former love Lola (mezzo-soprano), who is now married to the carter Alfio (baritone). Santuzza implores Turiddu to return her love, but to no avail. He rejects her violently and in a jealous frenzy she tells Alfio of Lola's infidelity. Alfio challenges Turiddu in the traditional manner (by biting him on the earlobe!) and in the ensuing duel Turiddu is killed, to the consternation of all the women involved.

Highlights are the wonderful intermezzo, played to an empty stage after one of the opera's most dramatic scenes and foreshadowing the tragedy to come and the Easter Hymn with Santuzza leading the villagers in a sublime and celebrated piece

and 'Voi lo sapete, o mamma' in which Santuzza pours out her
hear to Turiddu's mother Lucia .

Paul Dukas
(1865-1935)

First performed in Paris in 1897, *The Sorcerer's Apprentice* was a
great favourite even before Walt Disney immortalised it on
celluloid in the brilliant *Fantasia*. It is by far the best known piece
by Paul Dukas, who based it on a ballad by the mighty Goethe.
The tale concerns the adventures of a young magician's
apprentice who, in the absence of his master, decides to dabble
in a little wizardry himself. Using a secret formula he orders a
broom to fetch water from a well. The broom comes back with a
pail of water, dumps it on the floor and sets off on another trip.
The apprentice has forgotten the part of the formula that will
stop the broom. In desperation he seizes an axe and splits the
broom, but this only has the effect of multiplying the number of
brooms which are fetching water. Faster and faster they go, the
room is flooded, and the apprentice nearly drowned. In the nick
of time complete disaster is averted when the Sorcerer returns,
utters the right magic words and puts the apprentice and the
brooms in their places.

   All this is vividly described by Dukas, who thought of the
piece as a symphonic scherzo. The rhythms and the orchestration are brilliant, with the bassoon cast in a leading role with the
jaunty theme tune.

Enrique Granados
(1867-1916)

Although he had some success as a theatre composer, the musical
life of Spaniard Enrique Granados centred on the piano. He ran
a piano academy in Barcelona and was an international concert
soloist. In 1911 he played in public for the first time the two sets
of piano pieces to which he gave the name 'Goyescas', so called
because they were inspired by the paintings and tapestries of
Goya. Later he used much of the music for an opera of the same
name; it was supposed to have its first performance in Paris, but
the outbreak of war prevented this. *Goyescas* was ultimately

produced in New York in January 1916. Granados and his wife both attended and on their way home via Liverpool they lost their lives when the liner *Sussex* was torpedoed by a German submarine. The intermezzo from *Goyescas* is particularly lovely and well worth seeking out.

Franz Lehár
(1870-1948)

Franz Lehár was Hungarian, but for him Vienna was the magical city, the hub of the world's music and that's where he went as a young bandmaster. From the age of 30 or so he was able to devote himself entirely to composition and wrote 23 operettas.

The Merry Widow made Lehár famous but he had not been the first choice as its composer. He only took over when Richard Heuberger, whose masterpiece *The Opera Ball* was all the rage at the time, gave up the composition as he was finding it too difficult. Lehár had to do it in a hurry as the theatre in Vienna was empty and badly needed a production.

There was an air of gloom and pessimism about the theatre before the première; nobody was allowed in to see the dress rehearsal and the director, who hadn't wanted a work by Lehár, was heard to remark, "People will hear soon enough about this fiasco." One critic managed to sneak in through the stage door, the director begged him to leave but Lehár persuaded him to stay. It was just as well that he did, because after the rehearsal of the first act, the critic went to the director's box and said, "You are all idiots. If it goes on like this it will be not only no failure but a triumph such as this theatre has never seen!" Which goes to show that critics can sometimes be perceptive – and accurate.

When it did go on, *The Merry Widow* was not a smash hit but it wasn't long before everyone started to talk about it and it became a success, not only in Vienna but all over the world. It remains delightful and deservedly a great favourite, with a string of memorable numbers, including the celebrated 'Vilja' song. Lehár benefited greatly from his association with the tenor Richard Tauber, who starred in many of his operettas, including *The Land of Smiles*, whose most famous number is 'You are my heart's delight'. Tauber also played the title role in *Paganini*. Lehár was attracted to this subject because his real ambition was to be a great concert violinist. He studied and practised every day but eventually his good friend Antonin Dvořák could bear it no longer and told him, "For heaven's sake, nail your fiddle to the wall and try to become a composer."

"Without this advice," Lehár always insisted, "I would be a poor violinist instead of a rich composer."

The Modern Period (1910–)

Again, there's a little problem deciding where to start the Modern Period and who to include in it. Why, for instance, is Rachmaninov there and not Elgar? Well, Elgar composed the main body of his work before the 1914-1918 War, whereas Rachmaninov was only 27 at the start of the century and still had a very long way to go. However, there's no getting away from the fact that his 'Piano Concerto No. 2' (1901), with its sumptuous tunes, is one of the most Romantic works ever written for the piano. Some of the biggest names of the Modern Period are not included at all, because they just aren't middlebrow – Stravinsky, Berg, Hindemith, Bartok, Shoenberg, to name but a few. Actually, the composers who are included have more in common with the Romantics than with the avant-garde merchants. That's why they're in here.

The first major composer to break the Romantic mould was Claude Debussy. He was intent on creating a different kind of sound and wasn't interested in composing within the forms and structures of previous times. Impressionism took over from Romanticism – trends in music seemed to mirror what was going on in other artistic fields, particularly painting. Music went mad though, in this century. It has been the age of experimentation – what seemed novel and interesting at first became tame compared with later aberrations.

I won't go into detail about developments because a lot of them are of little interest to people who like to sit back and let themselves be engulfed by melody. To many modernists, melody is a dirty word, so that makes them alien to what we middle-brows hold so dear. I think a lot of composers in recent times have been outrageous in order to attract attention. Early in the 20th century, composers like Prokofiev and Stravinsky produced music that was dissonant and discordant, but they also showed that they could be Classical if they felt like it (Prokofiev proved it with a symphony) or Romantic (as Stravinsky was with some of his early folksy compositions). The people who indulge in electronic, microtonal, aleatory, concrete, serial and all sorts of 'New

Age' sounds have no place within these pages.

Some post-Romantic developments, though, are to be warmly welcomed. The introduction of jazz elements into "serious" compositions was exciting and stimulating. The Americans have been mainly responsible for this (Gershwin, Copland) but the French have also contributed (Ravel was jazz-influenced, as was Darius Milhaud some years later).

Folk music continued to be an influence in the 20th century. Of our Top 40, the Spaniard Manuel de Falla and the Finn Jean Sibelius constantly utilised it to great effect. The Hungarian Béla Bartok, though not included here, was obsessed with his country's music, collecting and editing it and incorporating it into his works. The Armenian Aram Khachaturian was another who was greatly folk-influenced. Closer to home, our own composers continue to draw from the enormous well of Irish traditional music.

I suppose we ought to remember that in every age, there were composers who were revolutionary and whose music was decried when first heard. Even Beethoven was criticised by some of his contemporaries for daring to be novel and "difficult". Berlioz and Wagner were denounced from the rooftops. The music of Debussy and Ravel was thought to be unacceptably dissonant. All these and many more liberals like them are now held in the highest regard, so perhaps people like Berg and Webern (both Austrian) will be the Haydn and Mozart of the 22nd century. For the life of me, though, I can't see Stockhausen, Milton Babbitt, John Cage, or any of the computer nuts being included in a later revision of this book.

CLAUDE DEBUSSY
(1862-1918)

Some would put Claude Debussy ahead of Berlioz as France's greatest composer, but they were so vastly different that they deserve separate billing. Debussy's objective was to liberate music from past conventions and traditions.

> *The century of airplanes," he said, "has a right to its own music."*

He turned his back on the forms that had served others so well, writing no overtures, concertos or symphonies. Instead he broke all the rules and resolutely went his own way.

Debussy was only ten when he entered the Paris Conservatoire, where he proved something of a problem to professors like César Franck. After collecting several minor prizes, he eventually won the Prix de Rome at the age of 22. This took him, like many a great name before him, to Italy for three years. In the meantime he had been pianist for a while to Nadezhda von Meck, the wealthy Russian lady who had funded Tchaikovsky from a distance for some years.

After some early wanderings, Debussy seldom left Paris. He composed mostly at night and became a familiar figure going for his afternoon constitutional – black-bearded, walking stick in hand to ward off undesirables both human and feline. He had an eye for the ladies and didn't seem too concerned about their marital status. He married two of his lovers, causing great distress to number one when he abandoned her for the wife of a wealthy banker. She actually tried to commit suicide and Debussy found himself deserted by many of his friends. He couldn't understand this – and felt himself grievously wronged.

Above all, though, his music was the great love of his life. It was not until his early-thirties that his individual composing style became revealed to the world with the successful first performance of 'Prélude a l'aprés-midi d'un faune'. Debussy tried to convey in music the impressions excited by scenes and events. Impressionism was the name given to a group of 19th century French painters, who set out to place on canvas not objective images but the subjective impressions of what their eyes saw. Debussy's aim in music was similar and he came to be described

as "the incomparable painter of mystery, silence and the infinite, of the passing cloud and the sunlit shimmer of the waves – subtleties which none before him had been capable of suggesting".

Debussy composed little during his last decade. He was 52 when the First World War broke out, and was deeply saddened by the events of the war, succumbing to a painful cancer condition while Paris was undergoing a heavy bombardment in 1918.

Debussy – A Middlebrow Mix

Clair de Lune (from 'Suite Bergamasque')

Debussy's piano music is particularly remarkable. One critic wrote of it:

> *No-one since Chopin so changed the character and tech-*
> *nique of piano writing as did Debussy...The new colours,*
> *nuances, effects, atmosphere created by Debussy brought*
> *an expressiveness to the keyboard it did not even know with*
> *Chopin and Liszt.*

The most famous Debussy piano piece of all – and probably the most famous of all his works – is 'Clair de Lune', his impression of the light of the moon and how it is affected by passing clouds. There are arrangements for other instruments, but stay with the piano version – that's the way Debussy would have wanted it.

La Fille Aux Cheveux de Lin

This is number eight of Debussy's first book of piano preludes. Like the poem by Léconte de Lisle which inspired it, the music depicts a beautiful Scottish girl with flaxen hair in the clear sunshine of a summer morning.

Another lovely piece from the *Préludes Book 1* is 'La Cathédrale Engloutie' ('The submerged cathedral'); from *Images* comes 'Reflets dans l'eau' ('Reflections in the water'). Also noteworthy is the piano piece 'Gollywog's Cakewalk', from *Children's Corner*, written for his daughter Chou Chou around 1906.

Prelude to the Afternoon of a Faun

When this work was first performed in Paris in 1894, the audience actually hissed. Audiences were much more demonstrative in those days – have you ever hissed or booed at a performance? Debussy had dared to be different, he had fashioned an eerily evocative impression of a poem by Mallarmé about the adolescent daydreams of a faun on a summer afternoon. Nothing like it had ever been experienced in music. This piece became even more celebrated or notorious when Nijinsky took on the rôle of the mythical creature, half-man, half-goat, in an erotic ballet. The music is languid, sensuous; close your eyes and let your imagination run riot.

Syrinx

This is a delectable piece for solo flute. 'Syrinx' is another name for the pan pipe, a primitive wind instrument consisting of a series of small wooden whistles.

JEAN SIBELIUS
(1865-1957)

We can think of lots of composers who died very young, but only a few lived into their eighties – Stravinsky was 88, Verdi reached 87, Saint-Saëns 86, Richard Strauss 85 but the grand old man was Sibelius, who attained the great age of 91. However, for the last 30 years of his life he didn't compose a note, even though he enjoyed a pension from the Finnish government which enabled him to live comfortably.

Sibelius was a national hero in Finland. Many of his epic works were based on Finnish legends and heroes. They caught the patriotic mood, being associated with the struggle to free Finland from Russian rule. The first of these was *En Saga*, but of course the most famous is *Finlandia*, written in 1899.

In his youth Sibelius roamed the woods near his home with his fiddle under his arm, absorbing the sights and sounds and playing as the spirit moved him. He also improvised well on the piano, though he said later:

> *I dislike the piano, it is an unsatisfactory, ungrateful instrument, an instrument for which only one composer, Chopin, has succeeded in writing perfectly, and of which only two others, Debussy and Schumann, have had an intimate understanding.*

Sibelius started studying law at Helsingfors (Helsinki) University, but his love of music took over and he transferred from the University to the Conservatoire. A travelling scholarship allowed him to continue his studies in Berlin and Vienna. Returning home, he taught music and played violin in a string quartet. He had five children in his happy marriage to Aino Järnefelt, a sister of the dramatist Arvid Järnefelt whose play *Kuolema* inspired the notorious 'Valse triste'. Another brother-in-law was Armas Järnefelt – one of a small band of minor Finnish composers (we've enjoyed his *Praeludium* on *Music for Middlebrows*).

Sibelius may not have used actual folk melodies in his compositions, but much of his music is nationalist in feeling – particularly the tone poems based on the famous Finnish epic the *Kalevala*. In his symphonies Sibelius aspired to be the Finnish Beethoven, concerning himself with universal problems, but his greatest talent was an extraordinary flair for conjuring up atmosphere – the romantic atmosphere of a near-Arctic and sparsely populated land of pine trees, dark forests and lakes, ice and snow.

Sibelius – A Middlebrow Mix

Finlandia

This great masterpiece was composed in 1899, a year in which the Russian government had just introduced some particularly repressive measures in Finland, including a curb on free speech. There was an upsurge of nationalistic fervour to which Sibelius contributed a patriotic tone-poem called *Finland Awakes*. As *Finlandia* it swept Europe and became indelibly associated with the composer. Sibelius himself was not too pleased with this as he felt that it took away from the attention paid to him as a symphonist. However, there was absolutely nothing he could do about the fervour of the Finns. The Russians got so worked up when they heard *Finlandia* that they banned it. The piece became a symbol for the Finnish fight for independence and later an un-official national anthem for the independent Republic of Finland.

The piece itself is not well regarded by the musicologists – not that that matters to us middlebrows! It's a great concert piece with a stirring introduction on brass followed by a lively section with percussion to the fore. Then comes the great emotional melody and finally a triumphant martial passage leading to a climactic conclusion.

Sibelius denied that he used Finnish folk melodies for Finlandia. He said himself:

> *There is a mistaken impression among the press abroad that my themes are often folk melodies. So far I have never used a theme that was not of my own invention. The thematic mate-rial of* Finlandia *and* En Saga *is entirely my own.*

The Swan of Tuonela

This is the most famous of the four legends inspired by the *Kalevala*, the Finnish epic poem dealing with such matters as the creation of the universe and the emergence of Finland from the cold northern sea. Sibelius used this epic as the basis for a lot of his choral and orchestral works. *The Swan of Tuonela* is a haunting piece for cor anglais and orchestra, of which the composer himself wrote:

> *Tuonela, the Kingdom of Death, the Hell of Finnish mythol-*
> *ogy, is surrounded by a broad river of black water and rapid*
> *currents, in which the Swan of Tuonela glides in majestic*
> *fashion and sings.*

Valse Triste

This was the hit tune of the day, but Sibelius made very little money out of it. It was sold for a pittance as incidental music for a play, *Kuolema*, written by his brother-in-law. This piece was to Sibelius as the 'Prelude in C Sharp Minor' was to Rachmaninov. He would gladly have de-composed it so that people would concentrate on his more serious works. One critic asked, "How could the composer of *Valse Triste* be taken seriously?" Well, Beethoven composed *Für Elise*, and some people take him seriously.

Karelia Suite

This music was written for a historical pageant at the University of Viborg and named after the region of Finland which inspired it. The tunes have a folk quality but are original. Most popular is the last of the three movements – a march which is full of bounce and has a melody which is instantly whistleable.

Pélleas et Mélisande Suite

The legendary lovers Pélleas and Mélisande have inspired a number of composers – among them Debussy, Fauré and Sibelius. One of the pieces Sibelius wrote as incidental music for a play produced in 1905 has become very familiar since it was used as the signature tune of Patrick Moore's TV programme *The Sky at Night*.

SERGEI RACHMANINOV
(1873-1943)

The aristocratic Sergei Vassilievitch Rachmaninov was born on a large estate in Tsarist Russia. He enrolled at an early age at the Moscow Conservatory, where he became a protégé and spiritual disciple of Tchaikovsky. As a student, Rachmaninov's gifts were compared to those of the young Mozart. His creative ability, it was said, bordered on the miraculous, and at the age of nineteen he took the great Gold Medal for Composition, the highest award offered by the Conservatory.

The future looked rosy for the young Sergei, but it was not to be all plain sailing. When he was only 24, Rachmaninov went into a deep depression. His colleague Alexander Glazunov must shoulder a great deal of the blame for this. It was Glazunov who conducted the first performance of Rachmaninov's 'Symphony No. 1' in 1897. By all accounts he had had far too much vodka by the time he mounted the podium, and the première was a disaster. The symphony was savaged by the critics, one of whom wrote:

If there were a conservatory of music in Hell, Rachmaninov would receive from it the first prize for his symphony.

The poor young composer took this very much to heart and went into a decline.

For almost two years he did next to nothing. He spent his time mostly alone with his pet dog as sole companion. It looked as if he might not compose again until he sought the help of a certain Dr Dahl, who by means of auto-suggestion or hypnosis convinced him that he could write a concerto of great quality. Rachmaninov did indeed succeed in doing so, and the 'Piano Concerto No. 2', which he dedicated to Dr Dahl, has become one of the most popular in the entire piano repertoire.

Rachmaninov was now really on his way and within a few years he was celebrated in Moscow as composer, conductor and piano virtuoso. He was made manager and director of the Grand Theatre of Moscow, and aligned himself with Tchaikovsky in opposition to the extreme nationalist school of the famous 'Five' – Balakirev, Borodin, Mussorgsky, Rimsky-Korsakov and Cui.

Rachmaninov toured the USA for the first time in 1909 with the 'Third Piano Concerto' as his centrepiece. He was a big hit and was never let off the stage until he had played the 'Prelude in C Sharp Minor'.

He received flattering offers to remain in America but put them on hold and returned to Moscow. However, in 1918 the Russian Revolution drove him from his homeland. His sympathies were uncompromisingly aristocratic and there was no place for him in Soviet Russia. Rachmaninov made his home in the USA and made frequent forays to Europe on concert tours. He died in California in 1943.

By all accounts Rachmaninov was not a bundle of laughs. He was inclined to be bad-humoured and was prone to melancholy. There is not much light relief in his music either. It is romantic, nostalgic and rich in luscious melodies. If you like to wallow in emotion (and I am not averse to that!), Rachmaninov is the man for you.

Rachmaninov – A Middlebrow Mix

Piano Concerto No. 2 in C Minor

The second and third movements of this concerto were completed by the end of 1900. Rachmaninov performed these in Moscow and, encouraged by the reception, added the first movement the following spring. The completed work received its première in November 1901. The piano opens on its own, gently at first but with increasing vigour until it is joined dramatically by the orchestra for the first theme. After a short development, the second theme is reached – it is dreamy and poetic. The second movement is serene and rhapsodic, with some beautiful melody being given to flute and clarinet. The finale is exuberant and exciting, with another wonderful melody being introduced, which was later popularised in the song 'Full Moon and Empty Arms'.

Piano Concerto No. 3 in D Minor

'Rach 3' has recently become much more widely known through being featured in the film *Shine*, the story of the eccentric Australian pianist David Helfgott. It has all the ingredients that make 'No. 2' so popular – sweeping melodies, luscious harmonies and emotional intensity.

Rhapsody on a Theme of Paganini

Paganini's 'Caprice in A Minor' attracted the attention of lots of composers – Schumann, Liszt, Brahms and, more recently, Lloyd Webber. (I hope he appreciates being mentioned in such august company!) All did variations on it. Rachmaninov wrote his Rhapsody in 1934. He was over 60 then and had been living in America for about seventeen years. There are 24 sparkling variations for piano and orchestra, making a piece which can rank with most concertos. The 18th variation is the famous one – it sounds more like a fresh melody than a variation – a lovely languid piece which is often heard on its own.

Prelude in C Sharp Minor

There are 24 preludes altogether, but why Rachmaninov called them that I know not. Each is a complete, attractive piece in itself, but the one that became a millstone around his neck was the 'C Sharp Minor'. It became celebrated the world over and no respectable music case was complete without it. Rachmaninov was never allowed off the concert platform until he had played it. There are all sorts of arrangements of the prelude, but go for the original version by a reputable pianist.

Vocalise

Rachmaninov wrote over 50 songs, but the one that has caught the public imagination has no words. It's a haunting, meandering melody for soprano voice and has inevitably been arranged for other instruments – particularly strings.

MANUEL DE FALLA
(1876-1946)

We hear quite a lot of Spanish music on *Music for Middlebrows*,
but most of it is by foreigners – particularly Frenchmen who went
south to visit and were much taken by the sights, sounds and
rhythms of Spain. Manuel de Falla, on the other hand, was a native of Cadiz in Andalusia, but he lived in Paris for about seven
years, enjoying the company of composers like Debussy, Ravel,
Dukas and Charpentier, as well as his compatriot Isaac Albeniz.
He listened to and admired a lot of music, and was certainly influenced by Debussy and his impressionistic methods.

Falla took his first music lessons from his mother, who was
a Catalan and he knew from the moment he heard a symphony
orchestra at the age of seventeen that he wanted to be a composer. He studied at the Madrid Conservatory, wrote a couple
of zarzuelas (the native Spanish type of short comic opera), and
in 1904 won a nationwide opera competition with *La Vida Breve*
('Life Is Short'). To his frustration the promised prize did not
materialise. Nine years later, the opera was produced in Nice,
Paris and, finally, in Madrid after Falla had returned there in
1914 on the outbreak of war. He completed *Nights in the Garden
of Spain* for piano and orchestra and also the two great ballets *El
Amor Brujo* ('Love, the Magician') and *The Three-Cornered Hat*.

After his parents' death in 1919, Falla moved to Granada.
He lived alone there at the foot of the Sierra Nevadas, a bachelor
and a devout Catholic. He was a painstakingly self-critical man
and consequently his output was small. He took the greatest care
refining and polishing his products before they reached the
public. His approach to music was conditioned by his great
interest, as a patriotic Spaniard, in the folk songs and dances of
his native land. It also reflects his devotion to Catholicism and
Church ritual and his great admiration of the 17th and even
16th century composers (the Italian Palestrina was the greatest
influence of that era).

Falla was a supporter of Franco during the Spanish Civil
War, though he abhorred violence and militarism. He became
disillusioned when the Generalissimo subsequently became
Spain's ruling dictator, and took himself off to Argentina where
he lived in a small town near Buenos Aires until his death in
1946.

Falla – A Middlebrow Mix

La Vida Breve ('Life Is Short')

In this opera there is a quality of youthful exuberance not found in Falla's other works. He was 28 when he wrote it, though it had to wait five years before being produced. It won the prize in a competition for one-act operas, but Falla later extended it and divided it into two acts.

The story concerns the love of Salud, a gypsy girl, for a local playboy in Granada. He seduces her and promises marriage. However, it transpires that he plans to marry a well-heeled girl of his own class. During the wedding celebrations Salud denounces her betrayer and contrives to fall dead at his feet (a good trick!).

The opera is short on memorable arias but is full of flamenco melodies and authentic Spanish dances, the most popular of which is known in its orchestral version as 'Spanish Dance No. 1'.

El Amor Brujo ('Love the Magician')

This is a ballet with the unusual feature of having a couple of songs for the leading lady. It's about a gypsy girl who is prevented from having any love life by the ghostly influence of a former, faithless lover. The phantom's powers are terminated in an exorcism scene which is enhanced by the fantastic 'Ritual Fire Dance'.

In the ballet the heroine sings or wails wordlessly over the middle bit, but we more often hear the concert versions for orchestra only. In fact, we hear this piece in arrangements for every instrumental combination possible. The piano version is effective and fun and often used as a recital encore. The 'Ritual Fire Dance' is weird and wonderful, evoking the atmosphere of a torchlit cave in which every shadow is laden with sorcery.

The Three-Cornered Hat

For some reason this ballet is hardly ever called *El Sombrero de Tres Picos* (except in España, I suppose). While he was living in Paris, Falla got to know some of the big names in ballet like Diaghilev and Nijinsky (and you couldn't get any bigger than these). Later the impresario Diaghilev commissioned Falla to compose a ballet for his London season of 1919. Leonide Massine was the choreographer and another Paris buddy Pablo Picasso did the decor. The only one missing was Nijinsky.

The ballet is based on a story by a popular 19th-century Spanish writer. It deals with the lighthearted adventures of a miller and his wife who is pursued by the amorous old governor of an Andalusian town. The music is strongly Spanish in rhythm and style and there is a very popular suite made up of three dances – 'The Neighbours Dance', 'The Miller's Dance' and 'Final Dance', which in Spanish folk terms are respectively a seguidilla, farruca and jota.

SERGEI PROKOFIEV
(1891-1953)

Sergei Prokofiev was one of the great originals of the 20th century. He managed to sound different form everybody else, despite writing in the forms that everyone else was using. He could be experimental or traditional. Some of his music is grotesque, discordant, intentionally horrendous, but there is lots more that is tuneful and easy on the ear.

Prokofiev was a very talented child and there was never a question of his pursuing any other career but music. He was a rebel at the St Petersburg Conservatory, where he was a student of Rimsky-Korsakov, and on his graduation he scandalised everyone by playing his own piano concerto rather than the customary Beethoven, Grieg or Tchaikovsky. His professors thought it was hideous, as did the audience, who didn't stay to endure too much of it. There were a few who recognised his talent and potential, one critic prophesing that in ten years' time the by-then famous composer would receive unanimous applause instead of booing.

During his twenties, most of Prokofiev's music was discordant. He ignored the old rules about melody, rhythm and harmony. He knew that contemporaries would consider his music "barbaric" but he didn't mind. That was the way he wanted to write. His 'Symphony No. 1' showed that he could write in the classical style if he wanted to.

In spite of being such a rebel, Prokofiev graduated from the conservatory with honours in 1914. Rimsky-Korsakov wrote on his graduation paper: "Talented, but completely immature." Three years later, just after the Revolution, Prokofiev left Russia and stayed away for sixteen years. He spent ten of those years in Paris writing ballet music for Diaghilev. He also spent some time in the USA but was disheartened by the reception his music received from audiences and critics. An exception was the opera *The Love for Three Oranges*, which was performed regularly at the New York City Opera.

Unlike Stravinsky and Rachmaninov, Prokofiev had not stayed away from home for political reasons, so there was no problem about his returning. He was welcomed back to the USSR in 1933 and settled in Moscow. Things went smoothly for him, his compositions were performed and published, audiences came to hear his works. The good things of life were made available to him, as they were to his colleague Shostakovich, who had never left. His works during this period included the *Lieutenant Kijé Suite*, the ballet *Romeo and Juliet* and *Peter and the Wolf*.

However, things were good in the USSR only if you played ball with the authorities. In 1948 Prokofiev, along with Shostakovich and several others, came under censure for the alleged "formalistic distortions and anti-democratic tendencies" of their music. The criticism of the state in those days was not something to be taken lightly. Some who resisted were arrested and came to a sticky end; others had to leave. Prokofiev decided to eat humble pie. He apologised for being influenced by "Western ideas" and promised to be a good boy in the future, using only "lucid melody" and "a simple harmonic language". He wrote nothing else of value, was rewarded with the Stalin prize for music, and died five years later.

Prokofiev – A Middlebrow Mix

Symphony No. 1 ('Classical')

This symphony was composed in 1917 and unlike many other titled classical works, it was christened by the composer himself. Prokofiev wrote:

> *I imagined that, if Haydn had lived to our day, he would have preserved his manner of writing but at the same time would have absorbed something of the new. That was the kind of symphony I wanted to write – a symphony in classical style.*

Prokofiev also admitted to having a secret hope that the title 'Classical' would prove to be accurate if, in the course of time, the symphony really did turn out to be a classic. I think he would have been pleased to know that his work is still admired as much for its originality as for its echoes of the old masters. It is bubbling with tunefulness and inventiveness and is captivating throughout.

The lively first movement immediately establishes the style with a melody in the violins that evokes a smile that will never leave the countenance. The second movement is slow and songful, and then comes a brief gavotte instead of the Haydnesque minuet.

(Prokofiev liked this tune so much that he later used it in the *Romeo and Juliet* ballet.) The finale is exuberant and brilliant, gaining steadily in momentum and having the wit and sparkling orchestration that would have brought a smile to Haydn's lips.

Lieutenant Kijé Suite

This was written in 1934 as a film score. An army officer is created by a bureaucratic slip of the pen. The Tsar takes an interest in the Lieutenant, so officials have to invent a whole life for him. The suite has five scenes, including Kijé's birth, wedding and heroic death on the battlefield. The best known piece is 'Troika', which ties with Mozart's 'German Dance' as the most popular sleighride ever composed.

Romeo and Juliet

Prokofiev was one of the many composers who interpreted Shakespeare's *Romeo and Juliet* in musical terms. One of the interesting things about the ballet is that initially it was given a happy ending. In the last act, Romeo arrives early, finds Juliet still alive and all ends well. The composer himself wrote:

> *The reason for this bit of barbarism was purely choreographic – living people can dance – the dying cannot.*

Later, after conferences between Prokofiev and the choreographers, it was found that the tragic ending could be expressed in the dance and so the music for that was written. There are some lovely dances in the ballet – a particularly lovely one being 'Dance with Mandolins'.

Love for Three Oranges

Prokofiev wrote his opera *The Love for Three Oranges* on a commission from the Chicago Opera, and it was premièred there in 1921. Three years later the six-section orchestral suite was an instant success, particularly popular are the march and the scherzo.

Peter and the Wolf

This is a favourite piece at children's concerts – but nobody is too old to enjoy it. It was commissioned by the Children's Theatre

Centre of Moscow and first performed in 1936. It's a fairytale with narration and has attracted many celebrated narrators including Eleanor Roosevelt, Peter Ustinov and David Bowie.

The story is eventful enough to keep young listeners on the edge of their seats and each character is illustrated by a different musical instrument with its own memorable melody. Peter himself is represented by the string section, his crusty grandfather by the bassoon and the wolf by snarling French horns. Other 'personalities' are the bird, represented by the plaintive sound of the oboe and the cat, who is signalled by the sultry clarinet. All ends happily, as fairytales should, when the characters come together in a happy march.

GEORGE GERSHWIN
(1898-1937)

The New York kid George Gershwin was roller-skating champion of his block in Brooklyn. His father had a variety of jobs, there was no piano in the home and not much chance for George to get a grounding in music. However, when he was six he heard a mechanical piano playing Rubinstein's 'Melody in F' and began to dream about being a musician.

At the first opportunity he took piano lessons and when he left school he got a job with a music publisher in Tin Pan Alley, pounding out other people's songs on the piano. He tried out little things of his own, too, and had his first song published when he was eighteen.

The big break came when Al Jolson made his song *Swanee River* a huge hit. It sold millions of copies and established Gershwin in the field of light music. With his brother Ira writing clever lyrics, he went on to write successful Broadway shows and film musicals, and his songs were sung by all the most popular crooners and big-band singers of the day.

Then in 1924, at the instigation of the bandleader Paul Whiteman, Gershwin came up with 'Rhapsody in Blue'. Its great success changed his outlook on life. He went to Paris and asked Stravinsky to teach him composition. Stravinsky demurred on hearing that Gershwin had earned about $100,000 the previous year and said, "It is I who should take lessons from you."

Gershwin continued to write the songs to keep him in the style to which he had become accustomed but he took himself more seriously. He wrote other works for piano and orchestra, including the 'Concerto in F Minor', which never achieved the success of 'Rhapsody in Blue'. Finally came his great folk-opera *Porgy and Bess*, which was treated with condescension at first by New York critics but which proved itself a masterpiece of enduring quality.

Gershwin suffered a brain tumour in Hollywood soon after *Porgy*'s first successful season. He died shortly after at the age of 38 though, as Mark Twain said:

I don't have to believe it if I don't want to.

Gershwin – A Middlebrow Mix

Rhapsody in Blue

This first saw the light of day at a concert given by the famous bandleader Paul Whiteman in New York in 1924. Gershwin composed the piece in great haste. It seems that he forgot he had been commissioned to do it and was reminded by a newspaper announcement just a month before the première. He prepared a two-piano version which was simultaneously orchestrated by Whiteman's arranger Ferde Grofé, himself the composer of some popular orchestral music, such as *The Grand Canyon Suite*.

The 'Rhapsody' leapt into fame and certainly realised Whiteman's aims of blurring the lines between jazz and classical music and with performances everywhere it established an international reputation for symphonic jazz.

Following Gershwin's death in 1937 Grofé expanded the orchestration so that the 'Rhapsody' could be played by full-size symphony orchestras and this is the version we most often hear today: though, indeed, there are many different versions and no two pianists seem to play exactly the same thing. As in all jazz, there is still some room for improvisation. A memorable performance in my mind was one given at a *Music for Middlebrows* concert at the National Concert Hall with pianist Philip Martin and the No. 1 Army Band conducted by Colonel Fred O'Callaghan.

'Rhapsody' opens with the celebrated clarinet solo which must be nerve-wracking for the clarinettist as it is totally exposed and sets the tone for the whole piece. When well played it seems to slide sensuously and seamlessly upwards until it flowers into the first bluesy melody and we find ourselves in the heart of music that follows no rules but is beautiful, agitated, sentimental, pompous – all when you least expect it. The critic Maurice Peress is worth quoting, I think:

> With one fell swoop of a clarinet George Gershwin in 'Rhapsody in Blue' launched his concert career in earnest. In its original jazz band format it stands as the most celebrated if not the first concert work inspired by the music of Afro-America and the form! A seamless progression from infectious ragtime through a memorable grand tune in the remotest key possible and a dancing return home via the Caribbean, the 'Rhapsody in Blue' is the veritable Rosetta Stone of the Jazz Age.

Porgy and Bess

As soon as George Gershwin read the novel *Porgy*, he wanted to base an opera on it but he had to wait while it enjoyed stage success as a play. Finally he got his hands on it and fashioned a work that was at first treated with condescension by New York critics but which later came to be regarded as an operatic masterpiece. The first New York production ran for 124 performances, which was short by Broadway standards, but incredible for an opera.

It is a tragic love story set among poor, Southern blacks. The principal location is the waterfront courtyard called Catfish Row in Charleston, South Carolina. It was formerly an elegant mansion but is now a tenement. The tragic hero, Porgy, is a cripple who has to propel himself around on a goat-cart. He falls in love with Bess and takes care of her when she is ill-treated by her man Crown. Later, in a fight, Porgy kills Crown but nobody is willing to 'help the police with their inquiries'. In the end Bess leaves for New York with another bad type Sporting Life (Sammy Davis Jr in the film). Porgy resolves to follow her and get her back, but we know it is a forlorn hope.

Porgy and Bess is crammed with more hit songs than any musical you can think of. There are wonderful love songs like 'Bess, You is my woman now', the celebrated lullaby 'Summertime', and Sporting Life's showstopper 'It ain't necessarily so'. But every number is a highlight and you should hear them all. There are also orchestral suites well worthy of your attentions. One is 'Symphonic Pictures of Porgy and Bess' and another is called 'Catfish Row'. There are terrific arrangements too, by Jascha Heifetz for violin and piano.

An American in Paris

Gershwin conceived the idea of *An American in Paris* in 1926 while on a visit to that city. Much of the work on it was accomplished at the Majestic Hotel – notably the famous 'homesickness blues' section about halfway through. *An American in Paris* is unusual in that it is one of the few of his works in which Gershwin did not write himself a piano part. He referred to it himself as "a rhapsodic ballet" and said that it was:

> *Programmatic only in a general impressionistic way, so that the individual listener can read into the music such as his imagination pictures for him.*

OTHER MODERN NOTEWORTHIES

Frederick Delius
(1862-1934)

Delius was the first English impressionist composer, just as Debussy was the first French. Born in Bradford in 1862, Delius showed a talent for music early on, but his parents had a business career planned for him and refused to allow him to devote himself to music: as a result he left home at the age of nineteen. He established himself as an orange-planter in Florida and spent his leisure time studying music.

After a few years he returned to Europe and made his home in the little French village of Grez-sur-Loing. There was a beautiful garden attached to the house, which was the creative masterpiece of his wife. She was a talented painter and much of Delius's music could be likened to impressionistic paintings of nature. Most of his works are pictorial and give the composer's impression of English country scenes. One of his most evocative pieces is 'On Hearing the First Cuckoo in Spring' or, as one confused announcer called it, 'On Cooking the First Hero in Spring'.

However, his early years were a struggle for recognition. It was mainly due to the enthusiasm and persistence of Sir Thomas Beecham that his work was brought to the notice of British music lovers. One popular piece edited by Beecham is 'La Calinda', which comes from the opera *Koanga*; it's a dance played at the wedding of two slaves on a Louisiana plantation.

Richard Strauss
(1864-1949)

Richard Strauss was born in Munich, his father being a leading horn player and his mother the daughter of Georg Pschorr – the city's wealthiest brewer. Richard spent most of his life composing and conducting music and making money thereby – it has been estimated that he was a millionaire by the time he was 50. Of his great tone poems, perhaps the most middlebrow is *Till Eulenspiegel's Merry Pranks*, which recalls the exploits of the rascally vagabond hero of a 16th century German folk tale. The piece is based on two main themes in rondo form, which run all through the music in various forms and disguises. One theme represents Till as a popular hero, the other as a vagabond and prankster.

Much of the early music of Strauss was considered to be the most discordant ever composed. However in 1911, with the opera *Der Rosenkavalier*, he changed his tune entirely and began to compose the most mellifluous melodies. *Der Rosenkavalier* ('The Knight of the Rose') was composed in homage to Mozart, but it bows the knee to Johann Strauss (no relation) as well, with a sequence of ravishing waltzes. Whether you ever listen to the opera or not, the suite of waltzes is a must.

Gustav Holst
(1874-1934)

If they had been making space movies when Holst was around, he would have earned a fortune. The man who has made that fortune, John Williams, owes a lot to Holst, although I'm not sure he admits to the echoes in the *Star Wars* theme.

It was a great idea for an orchestral suite – seven numbers, each representing a different planet of the solar system (Earth isn't included and Pluto hadn't yet been discovered). Holst was interested in astrology and he wrote brief notes to help the listener appreciate the musical mood he was aiming to create for each planet.

The first performance of *The Planets* was in 1918 under the baton of Sir Adrian Boult. World War I was still raging in Europe and listeners presumed that the opening movement, 'Mars, the Bringer of War', was a depiction of the warfare. Not so, however, as Holst had composed it before the outbreak of hostilities in August 1914.

'Mars' is thrilling and (dare one say?) ugly. There is a relentless rhythmic hammering that sometimes erupts into a horrific explosion. What relief we feel on the arrival of 'Venus, the Bringer of Peace'. This is slow and calm, a lovely adagio featuring harp, woodwinds and a solo violin. The final moments are ethereal, with the celesta gliding over flutes and sustained strings and fading away into space.

Next comes 'Mercury, the Winged Messenger', which might have served as the scherzo of a symphony and 'Jupiter, the Bringer of Jollity' has a glorious broad Elgar-like melody in the middle of the merrymaking.

Holst himself considered 'Saturn, the Bringer of Old Age' to be the finest movement. It is gloomy and mystical and suggests the ceaseless progression of time. 'Uranus the Magician' may remind listeners of Paul Dukas' *The Sorcerer's Apprentice* particularly as both pieces feature the bassoon. Finally, 'Neptune, the Mystic' uses a women's chorus, wordless and unobtrusive. Towards the end the voices become virtually inaudible and the music fades into the void of timelessness and eternity.

Maurice Ravel
(1875-1937)

Maurice Ravel remained a student at the Paris Conservatoire until he was 30. He was a first-class pianist and conductor and a master orchestrator, even giving others the benefit of his great skills as in the case of Mussorgsky's *Pictures from an Exhibition* (written for the piano). He was probably the most distinguished composer not to win the Prix de Rome, a circumstance which aroused strong protests in which his teacher Gabriel Fauré took part.

Ravel first came to public attention with the piano piece 'Pavane for a Dead Infanta', and much of his work was for piano. He was particularly interested in developing the possibilities of the piano and was as much an innovator in style and harmonies as was Debussy. The 'Mother Goose' suite of nursery pieces for piano duet is very popular, as is 'Jeux d'eau' ('Fountains') and 'Tzigane' is a great gypsy-style piece for violin and piano (or orchestra) with an extended introduction on violin only and the accompaniment coming in to build to an exciting climax.

Head and shoulders above everything in popularity is *Bolero*, described by Ravel himself as:

> *Seventeen minutes of orchestra without any music – one very long, gradual crescendo...no contrasts and practically no invention except in the plan and manner of the execution.*

How extraordinary that a piece so described by the composer should become his best-loved piece. It was actually written as a ballet for the Parisian dancer Lola Rubinstein and her company. The scene is an inn in Spain. On a table surrounded by spectators a woman executes a Spanish dance, accompanying herself with castanets. The spectators, at first calm, work themselves up into a frenzy as the dance reaches its climax. By all accounts *Bolero*, as danced by Lola Rubinstein in 1928, was the hottest thing in Paris.

Ravel, who had composed for a limited audience all his life, was thunderstruck by the acclaim accorded to this piece, which in recent years received a new injection of worldwide popularity when the English ice-skating team of Torvill and Dean chose it for one of their spectacular routines.

Bolero has two short themes, which are repeated over and over in a manner remarkable for the variety of instrumental 'colouring'. It is here that one might argue with Ravel about the lack of contrasts. There is no argument, however, about the crescendo. From a quiet beginning the volume gradually increases with electrifying effect until a dramatic key-change heralds the exuberant climax.

Fritz Kreisler
(1875-1962)

Fritz Kreisler was an Austrian, born in Vienna in 1875, and as a violinist he toured and retoured the world for years and years. His recitals would include the great classics but his audiences would be disappointed if he didn't treat them to a few of his own delicious trifles – pieces like the tuneful 'Caprice Viennois', 'Schön Rosmarin' ('Lovely Rosemary'), 'Liebesfreud and Liebesleid' ('The Joy and Pain of Love'). He would also play pieces which he attributed to 17th and 18th century composers, but were actually his own. He felt that in this way the pieces would have a better chance of critical acclaim and how right he was! Some of the hoaxed critics weren't a bit pleased when the truth came out. A CD of Kreisler compositions and arrangements (there are a lot of these) by, say, Itzhak Perlman is strongly recommended.

Ermanno Wolf-Ferrari
(1876-1948)

Ermanno Wolf-Ferrari was, as his name implies of mixed nationality. His father was German and his mother Italian. Although he died as recently as 1948, much of his music is reminiscent of an earlier era – particularly the 18th century.

When he was a boy he went to Bayreuth to hear the operas of Wagner and he was so deeply affected by the experience that he became ill (not, I suspect, the only person on whom Wagner has had such an effect). He also seems to have had a special affinity with the playwright Goldoni, perhaps because they were both Venetian, and five of his operas were based on Goldoni's plays. In fact, Wolf-Ferrari was chiefly known as a composer of operas, of which the best known is *The Jewels of the Madonna*. This became something of a favourite at Covent Garden after its introduction there in 1912 but has since faded out completely. However, some of the wonderfully tuneful music has been preserved in the orchestral suite, of which the best known piece is 'Popular Festival'. There is also some delightfully tuneful music in *Il Campiello* ('The Little Field') and *The School for Fathers*. And the overture to *Susanna's Secret* is a must-hear, the secret is that Susanna smokes on the sly.

Ottorino Respighi
(1879-1936)

Isn't it strange that Italian composers have produced a vast amount of wonderful operas but very little orchestral music of any significance? The outstanding Italian name in orchestral music is that of Respighi. We know him best for descriptive pieces, such as 'The Pines of Rome' and 'The Fountains of Rome', and for his orchestration of Rossini's music for the ballet *La Boutique Fantasque*. But he also composed an orchestral suite called *The Birds*, which was based on bird pieces by 17th and 18th-century composers.

He was a great man for arranging and orchestrating and why wouldn't he be, having studied with master orchestrator Rimsky-Korsakov? Well worthy of your attention are his orchestral suites of 'Ancient Airs and Dances', based on pieces originally for the lute.

Georges Enesco
(1881-1955)

Romania's leading musician for the greater part of his lifetime, Georges Enesco (originally, in Romanian, Enescu) is as famous for the fact that he was Yehudi Menuhin's teacher as he is for his own compositions. He was also a brilliant violinist – Menuhin referred to the "superb quality of his trills, vibrato and bowing", seemingly as effortless to him as to the gypsy fiddlers of his native country. Enesco lived for most of his life in Paris, but his compositions drew largely on the folk music of his homeland. His most popular work, 'Romanian Rhapsody No. 1', is an exciting piece; the music is original but the themes have the picturesque quality of Romanian folk music.

Zoltan Kodaly
(1882-1967)

In 1926 Kodaly had an opera produced in Budapest entitled *Háry János*. The composer described the hero of the work as "a peasant, a veteran soldier who day after day sits in the tavern spinning yarns about his heroic exploits". These include his personal defeat of the emperor Napoleon, a love affair with the empress Marie Louise, and his single-handed relief of Vienna.

Kodaly was a folk-music collector and made liberal use of folk material in his music, which includes some large-scale choral works, a symphony, and some chamber music. The concert suite from *Háry János*, however, guarantees that he will be remembered. The use of the cimbalom gives the music a real Hungarian tang – notably in the intermezzo – and the popular favourite is the *Viennese Musical Clock*, an object which arouses the wonder of the country-boy Háry when he visits the big city.

Jacques Ibert
(1890-1962)

The French composer Ibert wrote incidental music for a play called *The Italian Straw Hat* and later made a concert version under the title 'Divertissement'. The music is for a small group of musicians (probably all that was available in the theatre at the time) and some passages are a parody of the suspect sound that some theatre orchestras can make. The waltz is full of humour, with some intentional vulgarity thrown in for good measure. There is a march with a barely detectable quotation of Mendelssohn's 'Wedding March' from *A Midsummer Night's*

Dream and the finale is a circus type galop. This is music that will really make you chuckle and we can all do with a bit of that from time-to-time.

Carl Orff
(1895-1982)

Orff was an influential teacher in his home town of Munich specialising in the musical education of young children through singing, dancing and percussion playing. The composition, however, for which he is universally known, is definitely not for children. It's a setting of 21 medieval poems for soloists, chorus, and orchestra known as 'Carmina Burana'. The title comes from the Bavarian monastery of Benediktbeuren where the original manuscript was found.

The entire cantata is framed by a prologue and epilogue addressed to the goddess of fortune, who is acknowledged as the governing force of everyday life. The main body of the work is divided into three sections: 'Spring', 'The Tavern' and 'Love'. Some of the songs, particularly those relating to drink and sex, are quite raunchy but they're in Latin so who's to know? (Though it does make you wonder what the monks were up to!) There are some wonderful tunes and brilliant writing for chorus and large orchestra. The piece always has a terrific impact in the concert hall and the percussionists have a field day. The vigorous, swinging rhythms are a dominating force and carry the whole work forward in a torrent of all-engulfing sound.

Aaron Copland
(1900-1990)

Early in his career, the American Aaron Copland didn't seem to mind whether people liked his music or not. He won prizes all right and some scholarships, but little public acclaim. *The Boston Post* said, in 1927, that his Piano Concerto was "a concatenation of meaningless, ugly sounds and distorted rhythms". During the 1930s though, Copland decided to make a special effort to make his music more middlebrow, and he certainly succeeded with the ballets *Billy the Kid* and *Rodeo*. Aware of the use being made of folk music by European composers, he turned to traditional

American folk songs and dances. There are several traditional and recognisable cowboy songs incorporated in *Billy the Kid* ('Git along little dogies', 'Oh bury me not on the lone prairie'), while *Rodeo*, which was choreographed by the renowned Agnes de Mille, has the lovely 'Saturday Night Waltz' and the terrific 'Hoedown', which is the most popular Copland piece of all and is also often played as a violin solo.

Joachin Rodrigo
(1902-)

The guitar being the national instrument of Spain, it is not surprising that Spanish composers have contributed greatly to its repertoire. It started with Francisco Tarrega, who was born in 1852. Before him, the guitar was thought by most musicians to be an instrument good only for accompaniment. But Tarrega was a masterly player and his transcriptions of the works of Bach, Beethoven, Mozart and many others showed the great resources of the guitar. They also aroused the interest of other composers, including Falla and Villa Lobos, who were moved to write original compositions for the instrument.

The most popular work ever composed for the guitar is by Rodrigo. He was blind from the age of three but showed remarkable musical talent at a very early age. In common with a number of other Spanish composers, he made Paris his headquarters and in 1927 he became a pupil of Dukas, who influenced him a great deal. The famous guitar concerto was composed in 1932 and was an immediate success. Rodrigo himself wrote:

> *Concierto de Aranjuez evokes a great deal of colourful imagery and feelings. Being a history lover, especially of Spanish history, when I created this concerto, I had in mind the court of Charles IV, that Bourbon King of 18th-century Spain, whose summer residence was the palace of Aranjuez.*

The first movement is graceful and exuberant at the same time, showing that it is possible to strike a balance between the weak-toned guitar and the power of an orchestra. The lyrical slow movement accounts for a great deal of the concerto's popularity, and certainly lives up to Rodrigo's own aspirations. He said:

It should sound like the hidden breeze that skims the treetops,
as strong as a butterfly, as dainty as a veronica.

A lightly scored, vivacious allegro concludes this fascinating
work.

Aram Khachaturian
(1903-1978)

The Armenian-born composer Khachaturian showed no particular musical talent or ambition until he was nineteen. In 1922 he
went to Moscow and began the studies which were to lead to
great honours: in 1939 he was awarded the Order of Lenin and
the following year he won the Italian Prize for his violin concerto. In 1943 he had his name inscribed on a marble tablet in
the hall of the Moscow Conservatory. All seemed to be going
well but not long afterwards Khachaturian fell foul of the Soviet
authorities. In 1948 (together with Prokofiev and Shostakovich)
he was officially and publicly reproved for what was called "vi-
cious, anti-popular and formalist trends and bourgeois ideology"
and told to write in a more popular fashion so that the masses
could understand his works. Well! The masses have certainly
understood and appreciated his ballet music. He himself once
said:

> *In the best examples, this type [of music] has the ability to*
> *appeal to a wide audience and to win its respect and affec-*
> *tion. Without doubt ballet is one of the most democratic*
> *forms of art.*

He could have put it much more succinctly by saying simply:
"Ballet music is music for middlebrows." His most famous and
popular ballets are *Spartacus* and *Gayaneh*. *Spartacus* has that
marvellous adagio which became famous as the theme of the TV
series *The Onedin Line*. If you have been to any of our *Music for
Middlebrows* concerts you will have experienced first hand the
excitement of the Gayaneh dances, particularly 'Lezghinka',
'Dance of the Rose Maidens' and, above all, the celebrated 'Sa-
bre Dance'. Some of my own favourite Khachaturian music was
written for the play 'Masquerade' – the waltz is a must.

Dmitri Shostakovich
(1906-1975)

The Russian composer Shostakovich was alternately favoured and denounced by those who sat in judgement over the work of artists in the Soviet Union. His 'Ninth Symphony', for instance, enjoyed a wide and warm reception for a year after its first performance in 1945. Then suddenly an article appeared in *Culture and Life*, an official publication of the Agitation and Propaganda Committee of the Communist Party, sharply attacking both the symphony and its composer for their failure to "reflect the true spirit of the Soviet people". It was by no means the first time that things like this had been said about the works of Shostakovich. His opera *A Lady Macbeth* had been denounced as "bourgeois, formalistic, unhealthy and unintelligible to the people".

Shostakovich was a very serious composer indeed, but he did have his lighter moments and in them produced some beautiful melodies. One of them became very well known when it was used as the theme tune of the British TV series *Reilly, Ace of Spies*. It started life in the mid-1950s as a part of the incidental music for a Soviet film, and is the sumptuously expansive Romance from *The Gadfly*.

Samuel Barber
(1910-1981)

You will see references in these pages to the Prix de Rome, which has been going in France since 1803 and has been won by many famous French composers, enabling them to live and work in Rome. In 1920 the USA instituted a similar Rome prize and one of its early winners was Samuel Barber. He was a 20th century Romantic, writing music that was lyrical and easy on the ear. Not for him the ear-offending sounds of some of his contemporaries. He composed chiefly orchestral and chamber music but made his name early on with the 'Adagio for Strings'. This was originally the slow movement of a string quartet and was turned into an orchestral piece at the suggestion of the great composer Toscanini. There is a solemn melody which builds gradually to an emotional climax. It is a heartfelt piece which has become one of the best loved string works of the 20th century.

Benjamin Britten
(1913-1976)

Benjamin Britten was a child prodigy. He was only four when he started composing, which beats Mozart by a short head. The opera *Peter Grimes* established him in 1945 as a major composer, and he went on to compose a string of operas, including *Albert Herring*, *Billy Budd* and *The Turn of the Screw*.

He had a close relationship, both personal and artistic, with the tenor Peter Pears, who was his definitive interpreter. One of the works written for Pears was the 'Serenade for Tenor, Horn and Strings', considered by some to be Britten's masterpiece. Others would go for the 'War Requiem', a very personal expression of the futility of war. The middlebrow favourite is 'The Young Person's Guide to the Orchestra'. This was one of a series of works written in 1945 to commemorate the 250th anniversary of the death of the composer Henry Purcell.

This particular one was commissioned by the British Ministry of Education, and the alternative title is 'Variations and Fugue on a Theme of Purcell', the theme being a dance tune from the incidental music to *Abdelazar*, or *The Moor's Revenge*. It's a wonderful piece, highlighting the individual personalities of each instrument within the orchestra before they all come together in a final follow-the-leader fugue.

Leonard Bernstein
(1918-1990)

Leonard Bernstein has been one of the giants of the 20th century, a showman of unsurpassed versatility. As a conductor he had his detractors – some thought he was more intent on selling his personality than on interpreting the music. He was certainly flamboyant, but audiences always got their money's worth. He was an excellent pianist too, professor, television personality, composer and *bon viveur*.

His most memorable composition is the musical *West Side Story*, which ranks among the all-time greats. It's a Romeo and Juliet story, set on New York's West Side in the 1950s. The songs are memorable ('Tonight', 'Maria', 'I feel pretty', 'America', 'Somewhere') and have been recorded by some heavy-duty opera singers. My preference, though, is for the original cast or the film soundtrack. I just can't believe in Carreras or Kiri Te Kanawa as New York kids. The dancing is just as important a part of the show – Jerome Robbins put his stamp on it as director and choreographer. If you would like an orchestral version of the music, Bernstein has provided one, with the 'Symphonic Dances'. It's a masterful job of orchestration, giving full value to the marvellous rhythms and haunting melodies.

Another must-hear by Bernstein is the overture to *Candide*, one of the most high-spirited curtain-raisers you are ever likely to hear, and with a good main tune too.

That's all for now folks!

I hope that you have enjoyed *Music for Middlebrows*. Thank you for being with me and goodbye for now.